BUTLER®
BASKETBALL LEGENDS

BUTLER
3
VILLANOVA
4

BUTLER
BASKETBALL LEGENDS

STAN SUTTON

QUARRY BOOKS

AN IMPRINT OF

INDIANA UNIVERSITY PRESS

This book is a publication of

Quarry Books
an imprint of
Indiana University Press
Office of Scholarly Publishing
Herman B Wells Library 350
1320 East 10th Street
Bloomington, Indiana 47405 USA

Manufactured in the United States of America

Cataloging information is available from the Library of Congress.

ISBN 978-0-253-03526-4 (cloth)
ISBN 978-0-253-03421-2 (paperback)
ISBN 978-0-253-03525-7 (ebook)

1 2 3 4 5 23 22 21 20 19 18

All photographs courtesy of Butler University.

To Greg and Shari

CONTENTS

FOREWORD *xi*
PREFACE *xiii*
ACKNOWLEDGMENTS *xv*

1 HINKLE IS HOME AWAY FROM HOME FOR IU FANS *1*
2 BUTLER PROGRAM TURNS THE CORNER *7*
3 GRAVES AND GREEN: "FIRE AND ICE" *10*
4 IT'S A DOG'S WORLD AT BUTLER *13*
5 BULLDOGS GET A DUTCH TREAT *17*
6 BULLDOGS POUND WAKE EARLY *19*
7 SHARPSHOOTERS OUTSHOOT LOUISVILLE *21*
8 A NEW KID ON CAMPUS *23*
9 HELP IS ON THE WAY *27*
10 JUKES FOUNDATION SUPPORTS KIDS *30*
11 RONALD NORED STICKS TO STEPH CURRY *32*
12 BULLDOGS BREAK ONTO NATIONAL SCENE *34*
13 FOR CRONE, THERE'S NO PLACE LIKE HOME *39*
14 "PLUMP DOESN'T NEED A STUNT DOUBLE—EXACTLY" *41*
15 A DAVID-AND-GOLIATH STORY *42*

16 COMING DOWN OFF THE MOUNTAIN 46
17 BULLDOGS ARE IN THE FINAL FOUR AGAIN 51
18 A NEW ROLE FOR THE DAWGS 53
19 SOME DAYS SHOTS WON'T FALL 55
20 ALL IN THE FAMILY 57
21 MACK FOLLOWS HAYWARD TO THE NBA 59
22 LOOKING PAST THE HORIZON 61
23 JONES IS ONE OF A KIND 63
24 CLARKE'S STAY IS BRIEF, BUT BRILLIANT 66
25 JUST A HOP, SKIP, AND JUMP AWAY 69
26 BUTLER GOES BIG TIME IN THE BIG EAST 71
27 WORSE THAN A DEATH IN THE FAMILY 75
28 BARLOW'S FLOATER DOOMS HOOSIERS 78
29 IT WASN'T MILLER TIME 80
30 BRAD STEVENS IN DISGUISE? 83
31 CHANGES MAKE A DIFFERENCE 86
32 THE CITADEL TAKES A BEATING 88
33 BUTLER REACHES OUT TO BALDWIN 90
34 THIRD SEASON IS THE CHARM 92
35 DAWGS KNOCK OFF NO. 1 WILDCATS THREE TIMES 94
36 HAS BUTLER'S RISE AFFECTED IU? 97
37 NO ORDINARY ROAD TRIP 99
38 HELP FROM THE OUTSIDE 101
39 KELAN MARTIN STRONG IN ANY ROLE 103
40 X MARKS THE SPOT OF BUTLER'S BIGGEST RIVAL 105
41 DAWGS REACH THE SWEET SIXTEEN 108
42 LAVALL JORDAN TAKES OVER BULLDOGS 146
43 TALENT IS EVERYWHERE, JUST FIND IT 149

44 HINKLE FIELDHOUSE: A HISTORIC SITE *152*
45 BUTLER BOWL IS FULL OF HISTORY *155*
46 STEVENS LEADS BY EXAMPLE *157*
47 HAYWARD IN HIGH DEMAND *160*
48 "ON THE GROUND FLOOR OF INTEGRATION" *162*
49 ARCHEY'S 85 STRAIGHT FREE THROWS *166*
50 "YOU CAN'T TEACH SHOOTING" *169*
51 BULLDOGS FIGHT FOR RECOGNITION *171*
52 SIZE DOESN'T MATTER HERE *173*
53 HINKLE STARS AS NAVY COACH *175*
54 THE BULLDOGS' FIRST NIT TRIP *177*
55 BUTLER WINS A PAIR IN ITS FIRST NCAA TOURNAMENT *182*
56 YOU WANT TO COME TO BUTLER, KID? *187*
57 IU RECRUITS PLUMP AGGRESSIVELY *190*
58 FUN DAYS IN THE ICC *192*
59 PLUMP IS SHY OFF THE COURT *196*
60 DOWN GOES MICHIGAN *198*
61 "A TRUCK AND A VW BEETLE—NO MATCH" *200*
62 HINKLE'S CRITICISM IS SUBTLE *203*
63 BILLY SHEPHERD, SMALL BUT MIGHTY *205*
64 BEVO FRANCIS PLAYED HERE—ONCE *207*
65 TONY'S LAST GAME *209*
66 GETTING NOTICED BY THE OLD COACH *212*
67 BUCKSHOT IS A GOOD SHOT *214*
68 IU BACKS OUT OF HOOSIER CLASSIC *216*
69 TONY AT PURDUE? *218*
70 HINKLE AND THE ORANGE BASKETBALL *220*

71 NORM ELLENBERGER'S VARIED CAREER 221
72 A RUGGED FIRST ROUND 223
73 WAS DAMPIER DRIVEN AWAY? 225
74 ASSISTANT GETS THE JOB DONE 227
75 CHAD TUCKER IS STILL BUTLER'S TOP SCORER 228
76 OSCAR WAS *THE* GUY 230
77 REMEMBERING ANDREW SMITH, JOEL CORNETTE, AND EMERSON KAMPEN IV 232
78 STEVEN'S DISCIPLE NORED SHOWS CHARACTER AND PROMISE 234
79 BUTLER'S NATIONAL CHAMPIONSHIPS 236
80 BACK IN THE OLD DAYS 238
81 BENEATH THE HOOSIER SKY 239

ENDNOTES 241
REFERENCES 249

FOREWORD

STAN SUTTON HAS CAPTURED SO many great tales of Butler basketball, Tony Hinkle, and Hinkle Fieldhouse. Numerous people have played important roles over the many years, and Stan has gathered their stories. The coaches of Butler basketball have led the program with great care, appreciation, and awe. The players on the teams have given their all to fight for old BU. The Butler teams have always relished the challenge of taking on all comers, believed in the possible, and at times accomplished the seemingly impossible.

I hope that you enjoy the book as much as I did.

I wasn't born in Hinkle Fieldhouse, but I got there as soon as I could.

Barry Collier
Director of Athletics
Butler University

PREFACE

PAUL D. "TONY" HINKLE AND Butler University are linked by a short leash and a long history. For forty-one years, Mr. Hinkle, as most of his former players still call him even after his passing, held the heartstrings to the university's athletic program. He owned four titles at Butler: athletic director, basketball coach, football coach, and baseball coach. When university policy forced his retirement at age 70, his supporters tried to convince the administration that Tony should retain his positions as a part-time employee.

Several major universities tried to entice him away from Butler, but Hinkle *was* Butler. He liked cigarettes, white socks, and what other coaches would later call the motion offense. He landed good players because they respected him, not because he promised them the moon. He built a winning program around smallish guards, short but stout centers, and players that other coaches thought inadequate.

His home away from home—or is it the other way around?—was Butler Fieldhouse. On game nights the big barn on Forty-Ninth Street had a guest list ranging from maybe two thousand to ten thousand, if the Bulldogs were playing a national power. In his formidable years, a second half in the fieldhouse saw so much smoke in the rafters that it was hard for those in the cheap seats to see the court.

Mr. Hinkle died in 1992, at age 93, and to the end he could be found meeting his friends in a dark section of the building to talk over old times. When he retired in 1970, an estimated seventeen thousand family, friends, and fans crowded into the renamed Hinkle Fieldhouse to bid him goodbye. Each of them assumed Butler would never be the same without him.

They were right at first, but decidedly wrong in the long term. After almost thirty years of near stagnation, Butler basketball came alive again, attaining heights thought impossible for a small school. Butler became basketball's version of the little train that could. A succession of coaches, unlike Hinkle, found positions on other teams impossible to refuse, but before moving on they made Butler one of the nation's most popular college teams.

In 1993 the Bulldogs upset in-state rival Indiana University (IU), leading then coach Barry Collier to remark, "I think Mr. Hinkle would be proud."[1]

No doubt he would have been.

ACKNOWLEDGMENTS

I WAS INTRODUCED TO BASKETBALL in a rural Indiana gymnasium that sported only a few rows of seats on one side of the floor. The backboards, which were metal, hung close to the walls, and the team benches were on a stage. It was the home court of the Mays Tigers, who have gone by the wayside even as the tiny gym still stands.

The Mays gym was built in 1929, one year after another, more noteworthy gym was built on Forty-Ninth Street in Indianapolis. The modest 169-seat gym is every bit as important to me as the one that could (originally) seat fifteen thousand.

I'm uncertain who was the best to ever play at Mays. My sentimental choice is Don Dickerson, the Rush County scoring champion of 1951. Likewise, I can't even guess who was the greatest to play in Hinkle Fieldhouse. I'm partial to Oscar Robertson, but it may have been John Wooden or Larry Bird or George Mikan or Ralph Beard or Bob Cousy or Willie Gardner or George McGinnis or John Havlicek or Bevo Francis or Clyde Lovellette or . . . anybody.

"If only this fieldhouse could talk, the stories it would tell," said the late coach Tony Hinkle, who spent forty-one years coaching inside the building named for him.[1]

It is impossible to calculate how many superb men and boys played basketball in this fieldhouse—not only Butler players, but high school stars such as Robertson, who competed in the state tournament in the '50s. They came here each summer for the Indiana-Kentucky All-Star game. The Soviet National team played here, as did the Indianapolis Olympians of the National Basketball Association (NBA). So did the Harlem Globetrotters with Goose Tatum and Marques Haynes.

This book can't cover even a small percentage of the great stories echoing within Hinkle Fieldhouse, but its intent is to offer a wide look at the Butler athletes who played there. Many of these stories needed little research because they were already loaded in my memory bank. Many old and new friends helped enhance and complete those memories.

The Butler community was exceptionally gracious and committed to helping in so many ways, starting with sports information director John Dedman and his predecessor, Jim McGrath. Butler's archives of press releases, newspaper clippings, and pictures are housed in several file cabinets located in the sports information director's cramped office in Hinkle Fieldhouse. I am grateful that they were made available to me along with access to informed sources. Especially helpful were director of athletics Barry Collier and former coach Chris Holtmann and his assistants: Terry Johnson, Mike Schrage, Ryan Pedon, and Brandon Crone. Former Bulldog and No. 1 fan Wally Cox was not only immensely informative but delightfully entertaining. So was Bobby Plump, whose status in Indiana approaches royalty. Former player Nick Gardner couldn't have been nicer. Nor could Michael Kaltenmark, who keeps Butler Blue III "Trip" the mascot on a short leash and outlined the dog's life for me.

Special thanks to Ashley Runyon of Indiana University Press, who suggested a book about Butler and guided its production. Peggy Solis was always helpful, and Darja Malcolm-Clarke was a watchdog during production. My special thanks to Charlie Clark, who put up with my lack of technical knowledge and many other faults.

Going back to my time in the 169-seat gym, I must pay tribute to Marc Ellis, who died recently at age 95 while taking a wealth of basketball knowledge with him. As my first coach, he tried to pass it down, but at age 14, I figured I already knew it all.

BUTLER®
BASKETBALL LEGENDS

1 | HINKLE IS HOME AWAY FROM HOME FOR IU FANS

BUTLER'S HOME OPENER FOR THE 1993–94 season provided a special challenge for Bulldog fans who desired tickets. More than three-fourths of the seats in Hinkle Fieldhouse had been claimed by Indiana fans, and the red-clad Hoosier backers far outnumbered anyone wearing blue to IU's first game of the season.

"I've got a photo in my house, taken from up above, and everywhere you look it is red," said Jim McGrath, Butler's sports information director at the time. "I'm thinking, 'We're really playing a road game on our home court.'"[1]

Bob Knight's Hoosiers had the biggest following in the state at the time. The previous year saw them ranked No. 1 much of the season, with an injury to forward Alan Henderson possibly costing them their sixth National Collegiate Athletic Association (NCAA) championship. Two years earlier, Indiana reached the Final Four behind the talent of Calbert Cheaney and a roster of mostly in-state players. Entering the Butler game with continued optimism, and perhaps a touch of cockiness, the Indiana team still boasted a roster loaded with Henderson, Damon Bailey, Brian Evans, Pat Graham, Todd Leary, Steve Hart, and seven-footer Todd Lindeman.

Butler had already lost a road game at No. 19 Cincinnati, 90–72, and was coming off an 11–17 season under fifth-year coach Barry Collier. On taking the court that afternoon, the Bulldogs were aware that they had dropped six of their last seven games over two seasons. Butler had added Purdue transfer Travis Trice to the lineup, where he was paired in the backcourt with returnee Jermaine Guice. Chris Miskel, John Taylor, Marcel Kon, Matthew Graves, and Danny Allen also played extensively.

To the astonishment of all the fans in red, Trice scored 24 points and Guice added 19 as the Bulldogs stunned the eleventh-ranked Hoosiers, 75–71. The next day a newspaper headline read: "Trice 'n Guice Put Indiana on Ice."[2]

Knight was gracious to the victors after the game but was less so the following week as his team prepared to face archrival Kentucky in downtown Indianapolis. The Hall of Fame coach was especially upset with the six-foot-nine Henderson, despite his 13-point, 14-rebound effort. Henderson was 4 of 10 from the field and only 5 of 12 at the foul line.

Bailey scored 23 points against Butler that afternoon and the following week would lead the Hoosiers to a 96–84 victory over No. 1 Kentucky.

Butler continued on to a 16–13 record that season, and the win over IU probably provided the impetus for the Bulldogs to turn around a once-strong program built by Tony Hinkle that had been floundering for over two decades.

When Hinkle retired after the 1970 season, former Bulldog George Theofanis took his place. Tony's teams had won 560 basketball games over forty-one seasons, and Butler's home schedule reflected the respect that other coaches had for the Butler icon. For instance, John Wooden's powerful University of California, Los Angeles (UCLA) team played at Butler in 1962–63. Ohio State's 1960 NCAA champs played at Butler as did the

Buckeye teams of 1963, 1966, 1968, and 1970. Michigan, Purdue, and Illinois all lost at Butler in the 1960s.

"The fieldhouse had always been an attraction for visiting teams," said Collier, now Butler's director of athletics. "There weren't a lot of places that were as big and were the attraction that Hinkle was."[3]

Theofanis, who had been a successful coach at Indianapolis Shortridge High, coached the Bulldogs from 1971 through 1977. His Butler teams went 79–106, and visits by big-name opponents became more rare. Only three Big Ten teams played in Hinkle Fieldhouse in a two-year span, and by Theofanis's last season, a home-and-home series with city neighbor Indiana Central had replaced the larger schools.

Collier, who played under Theofanis, said one problem centered on the fact that Butler wasn't as good in those years as it had been. "There wasn't as much to gain by beating Butler teams for a while," Collier remarked.

Real or imagined, the administration's support for the basketball program dropped off until the team wasn't as competitive as it had been. In 1977 the coaching duties were handed to Joe Sexson, a onetime star at Arsenal Tech and Purdue and a longtime assistant with the Boilermakers. "Joe Sexson was a good coach," insisted Collier, not mentioning Sexson's 143–188 record over twelve campaigns.

Collier, who had built a solid reputation as an assistant coach at Idaho, Oregon, and Stanford, was hired in 1989 and had higher ambitions than the administration.

"We had some really lean years, more losing seasons than winning seasons. The program had really fallen behind, recruiting-wise," said McGrath. "We weren't getting top players; we weren't even getting top players to look at us. There didn't seem to be a great motivation to."

Collier hesitated to blame the administration but observed, "The support for the program had largely not changed at a time when the competition's support took off, led by the television exposure and all the things that had come about in the late '70s and '80s. Joe Sexson did not have the resources that I was given. I would note that Geoff Bannister, our president in 1989, had a vision that men's basketball could be a vehicle for the university to improve."

Collier, who would leave Butler after the 2000 season to coach Nebraska for six years, returned to Butler as director of athletics in 2006. Thad Matta replaced him and went 24–8 in his only season with the Dawgs.

When Collier first took over as coach in 1989, the cupboard was bare on the Fairview campus.

"Sarcastically speaking, we poured in six wins that first year," he said. "Six and 22, a really long year. Forty-four days between wins.

"I was most of the problem. My first year as a head coach could have been titled 'young and dumb,'" Collier added. "I don't want anyone to think that I wasn't the reason that we were 6–22."

Collier wasn't one to become discouraged, however, and saw light at the tunnel's end, even among the losses.

"I really felt like we had an opportunity," he said. "We were in a basketball area recruiting-wise. There were lots of good players, and we had a facility that was pretty cool. It needed work, but we had it; it was on campus and it was ours. And, we had an administration that had a vision for what it could be. I thought we would compete, and maybe I was naïve. I don't know, but I really believed that we could do this."

"It's unbelievable what he did as the coach here, and then coming back as athletic director. I think he was absolutely the right choice in both incidents," said McGrath, who retired after the 2015 season.

Collier believes the 1993 win over Indiana was one of the turning points in reversing Butler's image. McGrath also sees it as a major boost.

"It was definitely a turning point in the program. It was a point where we realized, hey, we can play on the national stage. We can compete with the very best. If you can beat Bob Knight in Indiana that's as good as it gets," he said.

At that time Indiana had won its last six meetings with Butler and fifteen of its prior seventeen encounters. As of this printing, the Hoosiers are 6–4 against the Dawgs and haven't returned to Butler's home court.

McGrath noted that, without a doubt, wins over Indiana mean more to Butler fans than beating anyone else.

"Those are the wins that always stand above all others. We could beat Duke and North Carolina, and we've beaten Carolina three out of six, but it doesn't match up to when you're playing Indiana," McGrath said. "Indiana is the number one game. Even beating Purdue is not the same."

The dramatic way the Bulldogs have beaten their in-state rivals recently has added to the significance of each win. In 2001 the late Joel Cornette dunked at the buzzer for a 66–64 Butler victory, and in 2012 the Bulldogs upset No. 1 Indiana in overtime on Alex Barlow's floater in the lane.

"Those are games that resonate forever," McGrath said. "They're exciting games anyway, and then to win like that puts your heart in your throat. People will talk about this game or that game, but it's always the wins over Indiana that stand out."

Collier credits some behind-the-scene meetings with former Wisconsin coach Dick Bennett as instrumental in the Bulldogs' turnaround. Bennett took the Badgers to the Final Four in 2000 and was known for his deliberate offense and rugged defense. His son, Tony, is the head coach at Virginia following a fine career playing for his father at Wisconsin-Green Bay.

"I had a really important event during the time I was coaching in the mid-90s when I met with Dick Bennett from Wisconsin," Collier said. "I went up to meet with the great man and Jim Larrañaga, who's now the coach at Miami. I wanted to talk basketball and try to learn secrets and those kinds of things. They had a philosophy and that really crystalized many thoughts that I had up to that point. I would say he was a key mentor in the mid-90s for helping us focus more on who we were and how we could be successful."

Collier and Bennett had met earlier when Dick's Green Bay team came to Butler and beat the Bulldogs 69–66.

"We played here at home on ESPN, and Tony Bennett speared us with about a twenty-nine-footer to win at the buzzer," Collier recalled.

2 | BUTLER PROGRAM TURNS THE CORNER

COLLIER HAD TURNED THE BUTLER program around within three years of the 1993 victory over Indiana. The Bulldogs would have winning seasons in each of the seven years before he was hired at Nebraska and former Bulldog Matta moved into the head job. The Bulldogs won twenty-three games in the four years after the milestone victory and posted sixty-seven victories in Collier's last three seasons.

Butler wasn't making much noise on the national stage, however—not winning its own conference tournament until 1997 when it made the NCAA Division I Men's Basketball Tournament for the first time in thirty-five years. The Bulldogs took a 23–9 record into their first-round game in Detroit, which they lost to Cincinnati 86–69.

Butler also made the NCAA field the following year, dropping a first-round game in Lexington, Kentucky, to New Mexico State 79–62. Then came its opening tournament game in 2000, when the Dawgs dropped a 69–68 overtime game to Florida on Mike Miller's last-second shot. Some controversy resulted over whether Miller got his shot off in time, but the Gators advanced all the way to the title game.

That was Collier's last game coaching Butler, and seventeen years later the loss still grates on him. "It's still hard to talk about it," Collier said, then talking to himself added, "Get over it a little bit." Nonetheless, the game got Butler a lot of national attention, if not sympathy, and some people believe it was another step toward rebuilding, despite the loss.

"We were the underdog, and I don't think a lot of people gave us a chance to compete with a great team like that," McGrath said. "And we did, we played them toe-to-toe. [Former Bulldog] Brian Ligon was from Florida and came to Butler because of that game."

Added Collier, "It probably put us another step closer. It was the third year out of four that we had been in the NCAA Tournament. It played a part the next year when we went in with Thad Matta as the coach. It was one of those buzzer-beater games that gets a lot of attention."

Matta coached only one season at Butler before moving on to Xavier. He was there for three years and then coached thirteen seasons at Ohio State. His lone Butler team thrashed Wake Forest 79–63 in its NCAA opener, building an incredible 43–10 halftime lead. Moving on to the second round at Kansas City, the Bulldogs fell to Arizona 73–52.

Matta's Butler team was blessed with some of the best talent the school had seen in several years. It included Thomas Jackson, LaVall Jordan, Brandon Miller, Rylan Hainje, Joel Cornette, and Darnell Archey.

Todd Lickliter replaced Matta in 2001, and during his six seasons Butler became a threat to win in-season tournaments. In 2002 the Bulldogs defeated both Purdue and Indiana while opening the season with thirteen straight victories. Despite a 25–5 record during the regular season, the NCAA selection committee ignored the Dawgs and relegated them to the National Invitation Tournament (NIT), where they beat Bowling Green and lost in overtime at Syracuse.

Lickliter's 2003 team continued to enhance Butler's reputation when it went 27–6 and sidelined Mississippi State in its NCAA opener. The Bulldogs then stunned Louisville 79–71 before dropping a Sweet Sixteen game to Oklahoma, 65–54. The Dawgs slipped to 13–15 in 2005, climbed to 20–13 in 2006, and set the stage for a bid to make the Final Four in 2007.

3 | GRAVES AND GREEN: "FIRE AND ICE"

BUTLER WAS INVITED TO THE preseason NIT in December 2006 by promoters who had no idea that the Bulldogs would win it. The pairings were set up with the likelihood that North Carolina and Indiana would be among the final four teams to play in Madison Square Garden. The Bulldogs would have to go through Notre Dame and Indiana in Indianapolis to make the semifinals.

Even though Butler had already scaled mountains in the early part of the twenty-first century, most people didn't realize that the Dawgs had two of the best guards in the nation and a cast of overachievers that wasn't afraid of the major basketball powers. In what would be Lickliter's final season in Indianapolis, the Bulldogs beat Notre Dame 71–69 and Indiana 60–55 to advance to the final rounds in New York City.

"If you look at it, we were part of the reason they took away that format the next year or so," said Brandon Crone, a senior on that team.[1] "That was set up for Carolina, Gonzaga, and Indiana. The setup wasn't for us mid-majors to be there."

After beating Notre Dame and Indiana, the Bulldogs sidelined Tennessee in the Garden 56–44 and then beat Gonzaga 79–71 for the title. The Zags had eliminated North Carolina in the semifinals.

One day after winning the preseason NIT, the Bulldogs were scheduled to play a home game against Kent State, which turned out to be a difficult double overtime victory.

Mike Green, a transfer from Towson University, became eligible that season and joined A. J. Graves in the backcourt. Graves had grown up a few miles from the IU campus but wasn't recruited by the Hoosiers. Two older Graves brothers had played at Butler, where A. J. remains the fifth-leading scorer in school history.

Green was less of a shooter but as tough as a three-dollar steak. He could agitate an opposing guard like a burr in his jockstrap and quickly became a centerpiece of the Butler system.

"A. J. and him, they were fire and ice," Crone said. "They had two separate games. A. J. was about speed and keeping his dribble alive and getting shots. Mike was about pounding the ball and toughness. A. J. and I played together three years. Mike had such a power game—a great passer with strong leadership. A. J. was the quiet assassin, just dribble around and shoot a three."

Added former sports information director McGrath, "I think a lot of people thought A. J. was too small. He was small of stature, an unlikely looking Division I player, but tough. Boy, was he tough. He could shoot it, but he could also handle it."

Green and Graves were supported by the six-foot-six Crone, Clemson transfer Julian Betko, Drew Streicher, oft-injured center Brian Ligon, and sharpshooting reserve Pete Campbell.

McGrath said Green was the glue that stabilized that Butler team, adding that assistant coach Brad Stevens was involved in his recruitment. "That was one of the best backcourts we've ever had," recalled McGrath. "We had a six-foot-six center who had a bad leg and really couldn't jump in Brian Ligon. We had a six-six power forward, Brandon Crone, who probably should have been a small forward. We had Julian Betko playing our small forward. That team was tiny but tough; boy, were they tough.

Then you would bring Pete Campbell in off the bench and he would light it up."

Former Butler assistant coach Terry Johnson worked extensively with the six-foot-eight Campbell on his shooting: "That was a weapon. The game could be at six [points] and it could be twelve in a hurry," Johnson said.[2]

Streicher was a weapon in the middle but only after he grew into the role. "Funny thing about Streicher," Crone said. "Drew was about five-eleven his freshman year; he came in as a walk-on. The next summer I was looking at him and he was like . . . well, I'm six-six and I was looking up at him."

McGrath noted that Crone was an extremely tough player. Same with Streicher. "There's a walk-on who's smart as a whip. He's one of the smartest kids we've ever had play for us," McGrath said of Streicher. "Defense? He got after you and just created havoc."

Butler continued on to post a 29–7 season and make another trip to the NCAA Tournament. The Bulldogs disposed of Old Dominion 57–46 in their opening game in Buffalo, New York, and put down Maryland 62–59 in the second game. That brought them to a 65–57 loss to Florida in the Sweet Sixteen.

"They had Florida on the ropes the last three minutes and a whistle here and a whistle there and the ball goes their way," recalled Johnson. "They could have gone to the Elite Eight or Final Four that year." If only they'd gotten a few breaks.

4 | IT'S A DOG'S WORLD AT BUTLER

BLUE III, THE ENGLISH BULLDOG lovingly known as Trip around the Butler campus, has claimed a celebrity status rivaling Lassie while serving not only as a mascot but as a major recruiter for the university.

Trip and his predecessors, Butler Blue I and Blue II, have given Butler a warm and cuddly image while not only appearing at Butler basketball games but also making dozens of personal appearances across the country. Blue II first stole the show at the 2010 and 2011 Final Fours when, by special exemption, he was the only four-legged bulldog to take the court. Fame was instantaneous. Before the exception was made, even fans of Butler's opponents cried foul when the dogs were banned from many basketball arenas.

"He can get into the US Capitol building but he can't get into the game," said handler Michael Kaltenmark of a publicity trip to Butler's game at Georgetown.[1]

Trip's visit to the Washington, DC, area in 2017 was made in his own personal vehicle, the Bluemobile, and paid for out of his own personal budget, all of which come from donations, sponsors, merchandising funds, and so on. Trip may make as many as three hundred annual appearances, most of which are for nonathletic purposes. Many of these outings are to the doorsteps of prospective Butler students, and in many cases his visits result in the youngster choosing Butler.

"When we go see a kid who's applied, they're three times more likely to wind up at Butler," Kaltenmark estimates. "I don't know that the dog is the reason but, obviously, there's an impact. I think the dog can take someone who's neutral and get him to take another look."

In many cases Trip will deliver an acceptance letter to the student's doorstep.

Trip, who weighs about 60 pounds, is decked out at home games in a blue letter sweater and has special duties at the player introductions. Butler's players pet Trip on the head as they take the floor, and the dog, usually barking, is trained to race to the other end of the floor for a reward.

"Blue II knew the drill. There would be someone waiting in the Dawg Pound with an oversized bone," Kaltenmark said. "He had that planted in his head. That's all he cared about. He wasn't going to forget it."

At one game his handler had Blue II and Trip on leashes. When he dropped their leads, he assumed both dogs would take off for the bone. But the younger dog noticed the Butler players jumping up and down and decided to join in the fun.

"Trip does a 180 and takes off for the huddle because he wants to be a part of that. Kameron Woods sees him and jumps back," Kaltenmark said. "By doing that he essentially singles himself out and Trip is locked in on him. Kam keeps jumping back and Trip is playing. He's still a pup and he's sort of snapping at Kam, although not maliciously."

Woods finally jumped behind a photographer, who grabbed Trip and ended the fun. "Kam might have been grazed, but I don't think he fully got bit," Kaltenmark said.

Trip isn't a nonpartisan mascot. As his handler said, "He knows the *Butler War Song*. He knows he's supposed to be doing something where he gets excited. He knows the word 'basketball' and he knows the word 'Hinkle.' He also seems to know, like if this is Saturday and we've got an afternoon game, as soon as I start to get ready he will never let me out of his sight."

The original mascot was a white female purchased in 2000 at the urging of Kelli Walker, who worked in the alumni office. The proposal was eventually taken to interim president Gwen Fountain.

"It went back and forth in discussions and, finally, as the story goes, Dr. Fountain said, 'Here's the money, go get that damn dog,'" Kaltenmark said.

Butler Blue I was mascot for four years, until Walker got a job in Washington state and took her along.

Kaltenmark donated Blue II, a male like Trip, and kept him in his own home on campus.

"That dog was fantastic. I took him to everything, including the office. I didn't really ask for permission to do it; it was just 'you can take care of the mascot' and that was it—a handshake agreement," he said. Blue II became known as "America's Dog" after dual appearances at the Final Four. He was retired in 2013 and died that August at age nine.

Blue II had been barred from NCAA Tournament games but was granted an exemption when the Bulldogs made the Final Four in Indianapolis. A major campaign on Twitter boosted his cause, and the following year, when Butler again reached the finals, he was also allowed in the arena.

At the finals in Houston, Blue II was called a "four-legged rock star" by the *Star-Ledger* and was the center of media attention.[2] One hotel even named a martini after him, Kaltenmark said.

Trip is reportedly maturing into the same manageable mascot as his predecessor, even if he did throw up once on the floor at Madison Square Garden. "You want to get some national attention, that's the way to get it fast," Kaltenmark quipped.

"Poor Trip. People see how young and rambunctious he is, and he gets a bad rap, but he's matured nicely, and I see a lot of things in him that I saw in Blue II. I like to tell people he's Final Four–ready whenever the team is."

5 | BULLDOGS GET A DUTCH TREAT

THE FIRST RECRUITING CALL THAT Collier made after he was named Butler coach was to the home of Eric Montross, the seven-foot Indianapolis youth who would become an All-American at North Carolina. Montross's father told Collier that his son had already finalized his college possibilities.

Thus, Butler's hopes of attracting a seven-foot center seemingly evaporated before they could solidify, but fortune was still smiling on the Bulldogs. After Montross enrolled at Chapel Hill, Collier called North Carolina coach Dean Smith and asked if he was interested in scheduling a North Carolina game in Hinkle Fieldhouse. Smith had a policy of scheduling a game in each player's home state.

"Eric hadn't even enrolled yet, but he said he wanted to play at Hinkle. He could have said he wanted to play at Indiana or Purdue or someplace else," Collier said. "So, they came in here in 1992 and gave us a haircut."

Nonetheless, Butler profited greatly from that 103–56 loss.

Rik Smits, a seven-foot-four Dutchman who was playing for the Indiana Pacers, took his visiting father to the game specifically to see countryman Serge Zwikker, a backup center for the Tar Heels. "He didn't play a lot, but he was one of four seven-footers they had on the team," Collier said.

"The next week I get a phone call from a guy who says his name is Ad Smits and he's Rik Smits's father. He says he's got a family friend over in The Netherlands who's kind of like Rik and wants to come to America to go to school.

I said, 'Is he kind of like seven-four?' and he said, 'No, but he's pretty tall, and when I get home I'll have him send you a fax.'"

Collier received a fax a couple of weeks later from Rolf van Rijn. "He says, 'I'm 218 centimeters tall and 99 kilograms.' Well, that doesn't mean anything to me, so I looked it up and said, 'Damn! This guy is seven-two.'"

Van Rijn came to Butler and made the All-Midwestern City Conference defensive team. Over a hundred and twenty games at Butler, he averaged 8 points and 5 rebounds while making 59 percent of his shots.

"If Eric Montross doesn't go to North Carolina, then we don't play North Carolina and Rik Smits doesn't come to the game with his dad, and we don't get Rolf van Rijn," Collier mused.

6 | BULLDOGS POUND WAKE EARLY

BUTLER 43, WAKE FOREST 10. Halftime.

The opening game of the 2001 NCAA Tournament was one of the most unusual in tournament history—at least the first half was.

Wake, a member of the prestigious Atlantic Coast Conference (ACC), never got out of the gate against Matta's Bulldogs, who made 16 of 30 shots and 8 of 14 three-pointers in the first twenty minutes. The Demon Deacons hit only 3 shots out of 25 in a pathetic exhibition of marksmanship while falling 33 points behind. They reversed things in the second half by making 20 of 34 shots, but the game was over long before that. The Bulldogs didn't really cool down, making half of their second-half attempts.

"It was one of the quickest halftime speeches Coach Matta was able to give," said Nick Gardner, a member of that team.[1]

Wake Forest felt the wrath of a motivated Bulldogs team after its last-second loss to Florida (69–68 in overtime) the previous season. "A lot of those guys had returned and they were ready to go," said Gardner, now Butler's radio analyst.

Butler was so good that McGrath was almost embarrassed by the Dawgs' 79–63 victory.

"The year before we had played in a tournament at Wake Forest. We weren't playing Wake Forest, but I got to know some of their athletic personnel," he said. "So when we played them in that game, it was good to renew old acquaintances. The first half is going on and I'm stunned; I don't know what to say. What do you say to a guy when you've got him down 43–10. To put that kind of half together on a national stage, I don't think Butler's ever had a half like that, and I don't think that many other teams have, either."

"Coach had us really well prepared for that game," Gardner said. "Coach John Groce had just come from being an assistant at North Carolina State, so he was very familiar with Wake Forest. We just felt very confident. [Teammate] Joel Cornette gave the pregame speech, and he had us all ready to go. We came out and jumped on them and everybody was making plays. I remember going to the locker room and thinking, 'What do we do to follow up?'"

Four of Butler's players scored in double figures, led by Brandon Miller with 18 points.

"I think the guys who had played the year before against Florida felt like they were owed one," Gardner said.

7 | SHARPSHOOTERS OUTSHOOT LOUISVILLE

BUTLER HAD WON EIGHT OF its last nine games when it went up against the Louvisville Cardinals on March 23, 2003, in Birmingham, Alabama, but few in the crowd gave the Bulldogs much of a chance. After all, Louisville had been to seven Final Fours, including four during the 1980s. The Cards had two NCAA titles and had been to the Sweet Sixteen twenty-one times.

Another Sweet Sixteen was up for grabs against Butler. But this time the Cardinals had to contend with Darnell Archey, who hit eight of his nine three-point attempts as the Bulldogs eliminated Louisville 79–71. Archey led the Dawgs with 26 points, and Mike Monserez scored 14 points while making four of seven three-pointers.

"We came off a real low-scoring game in the first round against Mississippi State [47–46]. Louisville was a much more open game," said Gardner. "Darnell Archey got hot, so we were riding his hand. We were making shots all over the floor. Our staff had us really well prepared."

Archey is one of Butler's great all-time shooters, comparing well with Pete Campbell, Rotnei Clarke, A. J. Graves, Kellen Dunham, and others.

"Darnell was one of those guys. He just worked on it. The guy lived in the gym; he'd come back in the evening and get shots up. He tried to master his craft," Gardner said. "If you can shoot the ball at that level, you change the way defenses have to guard you."

After beating Louisville, Lickliter's Bulldogs lost to Oklahoma in the Sweet Sixteen.

8 | A NEW KID ON CAMPUS

DURING THE SUMMER OF 2000, a 23-year-old DePauw University graduate decided on a career change that would be one of the most successful since Ronald Reagan left the movies for politics.

Bradley Kent Stevens had converted an economics degree into a pharmaceutical position at one of Indiana's most prestigious firms, Eli Lilly. Described as extremely bright with a work ethic at the highest level, Brad had a rosy future in business as well as a longtime girlfriend who supported what some would have considered a crazy notion.

Stevens had set four school records as a basketball player at Zionsville High School near Indianapolis and was a four-year letterman at DePauw. He realized that he had maximized his on-court achievements but still retained a serious itch for the game. Having worked at Butler's summer basketball camps, he was offered a volunteer position in Butler's basketball office. Collier had taken the coaching job at Nebraska at this point, and assistant Matta had moved up.

At the time Stevens was a year out of college and his girlfriend, Tracy Wilhelmy, returned to DePauw to get her law degree as insurance against Brad's trifling opening salary at Butler.

A year later Matta became head coach at Xavier and new coach Lickliter promoted Brad to a full-time assistant coach. In that role Stevens revealed the drive and inner basketball savvy that left a strong impression on his superiors.

Butler's renewed basketball success had made its head coaches viable candidates for positions at larger schools. Butler was still in the Horizon League, and it remained a mid-major program, but Collier and Matta were hired away, and Lickliter's star continued to rise, especially after the Bulldogs won twenty-nine games in 2007 and reached the Sweet Sixteen.

Then, Lickliter was hired to coach the Iowa Hawkeyes, and for the third time in eight years, Butler needed to replace its head coach.

Collier had returned to the program as director of athletics by then, and the players met with him to urge an in-house promotion. Collier was a hands-on athletic director, closely observing practices and evaluating the assistants. The three assistants were interviewed for the position, and within hours Collier hired Stevens.

Many Butler fans didn't even recognize the name of the new 31-year-old head coach, who looked even younger. Any complaints were dismissed after the Bulldogs won their first eight games, including the Great Alaska Shootout title in which the Dawgs beat Michigan, Virginia Tech, and Bob Knight's Texas Tech team. The Bulldogs also beat Ohio State 65–46 with a second-half blitz of three-pointers.

"You understand when you hear Brad that he is one of the great communicators I have ever known," Collier said. "He can speak to 3-year-olds and 103-year-olds, whatever the scenario is. College kids and professional athletes, donors and parents. He is a tremendous communicator. Those things are pretty rare to have at such a high level."

Stevens was fortunate to inherit a veteran team led by guards Graves and Green. After the Bulldogs finally lost at Wright State, they won their next eight games, including a victory over Florida State of the always tough ACC. They also won a two-point game at Southern Illinois when Graves buried a three-pointer from the backcourt in the final second.

Butler closed Stevens's first season with a 30–4 record, beating South Alabama 81–61 in the NCAA Tournament before losing to Tennessee in overtime.

"I thought Brad would be a really good coach, but did I think he'd be 30–4 his first year and be one of the best coaches ever? No, I didn't think that," Collier admitted.

Even after Stevens left in 2013 to coach the Boston Celtics, Butler's succession of coaches have continued to excel, largely due to Collier's astute choices.

"The system obviously has worked," said McGrath. "Thad Matta carried it out, Todd Lickliter did. Brad Stevens. Chris Holtmann. Every one of them has followed in the same philosophy that Barry put in place. When Barry left, I thought, 'Boy, that's a great loss to us,' but I knew Thad understood what Barry was doing.

"I didn't know if Thad could build on it, but he immediately did. And then he left and Todd Lickliter took over and took things to another level. Then he leaves and I'm thinking, maybe we've hit our pinnacle, and then a guy named Brad Stevens steps in and just changes everything."

Everyone around Stevens agrees on his strong points, which include a calm demeanor, great communication skills, and hard work.

Describing his reasons for promoting Stevens, Collier said, "I saw somebody whose integrity was value-based. He had learned our system from the inside; although he was young, he had good experience here at Butler under good coaches. He is extremely bright, but what you might not know about is he has a great motor. He is a high-energy guy; he might not show it, but he's flapping like crazy under the water."

Added McGrath, "Brad did it with such grace. He always treated people unbelievably. He is as good a person as I've ever met. He would do anything for anybody."

9 | HELP IS ON THE WAY

BUTLER'S BRILLIANCE IN BRAD STEVENS'S debut season wasn't totally unexpected because his first team had both experience and talent. Green and Graves were seniors, as were Betko, Streicher, and Campbell. For the next season, Stevens would have to build around Matt Howard, who had become a starter as a freshman and displayed an energy that rubbed off on his teammates. Willie Veasley, a strong defender, sharpshooting Zach Hahn, and Alabama transfer Avery Jukes had also played for Stevens's first team, but the second-year coach would need a strong recruiting class to post another good season.

The class that Stevens brought in would be the strongest in school history, one that included two current NBA players and two others who would lead the Bulldogs to back-to-back national championship games. Gordon Hayward and Shelvin Mack were so good they turned pro early, and Ronald Nored and Shawn Vanzant played major roles in Butler's advancement. The class also included Garrett Butcher, whose career would be stymied by injuries.

A product of nearby Brownsburg High, Hayward had stood only five-eleven as a high school freshman. His early basketball experiences were as a guard, and when his height soared to six-eight, he still had backcourt skills. Gordon also excelled in tennis, which improved his footwork on the court.[1]

Purdue and Indiana University–Purdue University Indianapolis (IUPUI) were the only other schools to offer him a scholarship, partly because he bypassed Athletic Amateur Union (AAU) basketball to concentrate on tennis. Also, his boyish, floppy-haired appearance didn't project him as a blue-chip player.

Collier recalled a remark by Kokomo High coach Basil Mawbey:

"He was a basketball lifer and he came to a preseason workout before Gordon's freshman year," Collier recounted. "And he said, 'That kid's going to be a pro.' I'll never forget that. Basil nailed that one."

Former Butler assistant coach Johnson said Hayward's and Mack's talents weren't totally recognized until they were standouts on a USA team the summer after their freshman season.

"We began hearing rumblings about Gordon being the best player on the floor," Johnson said. "We thought, 'Well, we may have an NBA guy.' NBA guys were talking about him. We thought we may lose him. We go to Italy and play against the Yugoslavia National team. There was an NBA player on that team, and Gordon and him just went at it. It was fun to watch."

McGrath recalled the arrival of the Hayward-Mack class. "When Brad recruited those guys, we knew they were good players, but I don't know that we saw them as future NBA players," McGrath said. "We thought they were guys who fit our program, fit our style. We thought maybe they could improve our level a little, but they turned out to be so much more than anybody had ever imagined."

The recruiting of Mack out of Lexington, Kentucky, stunned many fans for two reasons: Butler had no history of recruiting that city, and Mack's statistics made him very attractive to the Kentucky Wildcats. As a senior at Bryan Station High, Mack averaged 24 points, 8 rebounds, 8 assists, and 4 steals a game. Butler started recruiting him early and beat Kentucky to the punch.

Nored also had a Kentucky connection, although he was from Alabama. He had given a verbal commitment to play at Western Kentucky, but when Hilltoppers coach Darrin Horn left to coach South Carolina, Nored opted for Butler, located close to his grandparents' house. Nored had turned down an academic scholarship to Harvard and was elected president of the freshman class at Butler.

"The catalyst for the whole group was Matt Howard," McGrath said of that class. "He really, really made them jell. The others brought talent; they brought individual skills, but Matt Howard brought the whole thing together. He was one of the most amazing players I've ever seen."

Howard, who had been an All-State forward at Connersville High, had a high energy level and excelled at the college game. He had an early season double-double against Michigan, and he quickly worked his way into the starting lineup for the next four years.

Stevens's second team began the 2008–09 season with eight victories, finally losing at Ohio State 54–51 before winning another fifteen in a row. The Bulldogs won the Horizon League en route to a 26–6 record that included a first-round loss to Louisiana State University (LSU) in the NCAA Tournament.[1]

10 | JUKES FOUNDATION SUPPORTS KIDS

AVERY JUKES WILL BE REMEMBERED as the backup center on Butler's 2010 national runner-up team. In a remote nation in Africa, he will be remembered as a great humanitarian.

The six-foot-eight Jukes, a Georgia native who transferred to Butler from Alabama in January 2007, made his biggest contribution to the Bulldogs by scoring 10 points in the first half of the title game against Duke. As he had in several games that season, Avery came to the rescue when starter Howard encountered foul trouble.

Jukes had played part of one season for the Crimson Tide before changing schools. In his initial season with the Bulldogs, he made 60 percent of his shots, including 60 percent on three-point attempts, and offered a big body to compete within the top levels of college basketball.

But his contribution to mankind came as a result of an eleven-day missions trip with Ambassadors for Children to Uganda in the summer of 2008. Jukes and fifteen other students helped build a school, and while there, he was touched by the young people of that nation. On returning home, he founded the Avery Jukes Foundation for Kids to support the young people of Uganda. His foundation launched a successful drive to provide books for the Uganda children.

The money raised through Avery's foundation helped Ugandan young people attend secondary schools.

"Our mission is to make a global impact by helping kids around the world to receive food, clothing and a suitable education," Jukes said in a prepared statement through Butler.

As a youth, Jukes helped lead South Gwinnett High School to the 2004 Class AAAAA Georgia State Championship.

11 | RONALD NORED STICKS TO STEPH CURRY

BRACKETBUSTER BASKETBALL GAMES WERE CREATED as a made-for-television attraction to air a few weeks before the NCAA Tournament. ESPN popularized the concept, which in 2009 involved mid-major teams from a number of conferences, including the Horizon League. The BracketBuster games were scheduled later in the evening than other games and were seen as an opportunity for smaller schools to get national visibility and improve their chances of making the national championship.

On February 21, 2009, Butler was scheduled to play a BracketBuster road game at Davidson College. Davidson's freshman-oriented team had posted a 22–4 record. The Dawgs made the trip coming off successive close losses to Loyola and Milwaukee. The prior season Butler had dropped a BracketBuster to Drake University in Indianapolis.

Davidson presented a special challenge because it had an All-American, a six-foot-three senior guard named Stephen Curry, whose father, Dell, had been a standout at Virginia Tech. Steph had grown up shooting goals with his younger brother, Seth, and the Charlotte Hornets of the NBA, for whom his father played. He wanted to play collegiately at Virginia Tech, but the Hokies only offered him a chance as a nonscholarship player. Weighing only 160 pounds, he enrolled at Davidson near his Charlotte, North Carolina, home.

One week before the Butler game, Curry scored his two thousandth point for Davidson. Butler would need someone to guard the slender hotshot who would ultimately lead all Division I scorers and drain 414 three-pointers as a collegian.

That player would be freshman Nored, the Bulldogs' principal defender on a team of great defenders. Nored was up to the task, proving unshakeable to the Davidson star as Butler posted a 75–63 victory. Curry played thirty-seven minutes, the same as Nored, and struggled mightily to score 20 points, which was 9 under his average. Nored, with the help of his teammates, limited him to six baskets in 23 shots. The Davidson star made only two of his thirteen three-point attempts, and Nored's pressure defense was instrumental in Curry committing seven of his team's nineteen turnovers.

In terms of scoring in that game, Curry was upstaged by future professional rival Hayward, who scored 27 points. Curry went on to a brilliant career in the NBA, becoming the league's most valuable player (MVP) in 2015 and 2016.

12 | BULLDOGS BREAK ONTO NATIONAL SCENE

FOLLOWING A 56–10 RECORD OVER his first two seasons, Stevens was ready to make his mark on college basketball in 2009–10. The season got off to a strong start with victories over Davidson, Northwestern, and University of Evansville, but losses to No. 22 Minnesota, No. 19 Clemson, and No. 13 Georgetown dotted a tough December schedule. Butler had an 8–3 record when it traveled to University of Alabama-Birmingham (UAB) on December 22.

The Bulldogs lost by 10 points to the Blazers but didn't lose again until April, in the two-point heartbreaker for the national championship. The Bulldogs rolled past all eighteen opponents in the Horizon League, adding wins over Milwaukee and Wright State in the conference tournament. In the only out-of-league game since the loss to UAB, the Dawgs buried Siena College in a BracketBuster game. Hayward was named Horizon Player of the Year, succeeding Howard, and Hayward, Howard, and Mack were All-Horizon first team.

As expected, the Bulldogs were the only team from the Horizon League to make the sixty-five-team NCAA field. Butler was given the No. 5 seed, a spot that had proved vulnerable against

No. 12 in prior tournaments. As a result, many people familiar with that trend picked the Dawgs to drop their first-round game against University of Texas at El Paso (UTEP).

The Bulldogs were shipped to the West Regional site in San Jose, California, the most distant site for their fans, but a large traveling party followed. The four No. 1 seeds included Syracuse (28–4) in the West, Kentucky (32–2) in the East, Kansas (32–2) in the Midwest, and Duke (32–2) in the South.

Butler was tested until halftime but put away the Miners in the second half 77–59 as Mack completed a 25-point performance. No. 4 seed Vanderbilt was in the adjacent bracket but was upset by Ohio Valley Conference champion Murray State, 66–65. Danero Thomas's basket at the buzzer propelled the Racers into the second round.

Butler's second game proved to be the Bulldogs' toughest win of the tournament. Nored made a crucial three-pointer, and Hayward batted away a Murray State pass in the closing seconds as the Dawgs advanced to the Sweet Sixteen with a 54–52 triumph.

Back home for a week before going to Salt Lake City to play favored Syracuse, the Bulldogs prepared for their first trip to the Sweet Sixteen in three years. The Orange had advanced with a 79–56 win over Vermont and an 87–65 victory over Gonzaga. Their vaunted zone defense promised to be a challenge for the Dawgs, who nonetheless jumped out of the gate and took a 12–2 lead after seven minutes. By halftime the Dawgs had a 35–25 advantage.

Butler's defensive strength forced the Orange into five turnovers during the opening seven minutes and a total of eighteen in the game. Syracuse coach Jim Boeheim later bemoaned the fact that his team had never made that many errors but, of course, creating turnovers was a Butler trademark.

Hayward led the Bulldogs with 17 points in their 63–59 victory. Syracuse took a four-point lead in the second half, but Nored made a rare, and critical, three-pointer to pull the Dawgs within a point at 3:09 on the clock. Veasley, like Nored a defensive fixture for Butler, also hit a late shot from the left corner that bounced high off the basket and fell through. Butler's defense, which didn't allow an opponent more than 59 points until the national title game, held Syracuse scoreless for nearly the final five minutes.

Kansas State, seeded second in the West, outlasted No. 6 Xavier 101–96 in double overtime for the right to play Butler in the Elite Eight game. Butler owned a one-point victory over Xavier during the season. The Wildcats overcame 32 points by Jordan Crawford in the semifinal, and Xavier's Terrell Holloway tied the game with three foul shots at 0:05 of regulation.

Kansas State (26–7) was taller than Butler, but the rebounding was even as the Bulldogs dominated much of the game, although not putting it away until the final two minutes, 63–56. The Bulldogs moved ahead 14–7 and doubled the score 20–10 with backup centers Andrew Smith and Avery Jukes getting baskets while a foul-prone Howard rode the bench.

Butler's halftime lead was 27–20, and Mack's fifteen-footer with 7:30 to play made the margin 49–39. Kansas State battled back to 56–54 with 2:40 to play, but Nored, shining again at a critical moment, drove the lane for a score. Hayward's bucket, giving him 22 points, provided some cushion.

The victory marked Butler's first trip to the Final Four with the additional thrill of playing in Lucas Oil Stadium in Indianapolis. Hayward and Mack were named to the All-West Regional team.

Final Four opponent Michigan State University (MSU) had played in Lucas Oil the previous season, beating Louisville in the regional en route to the Final Four in Detroit. Butler's campus is across town from the Final Four site, and the city of Indianapolis was abuzz with emotion throughout the week.

Like Butler, MSU carried a No. 5 seed into the tournament, which it opened with a 70–67 victory over New Mexico State. The Spartans, 24–8 on the regular season, then had to go all out to get by fourth-seeded Maryland, 85–83. Advancing to the Midwest Regional in St. Louis, Tom Izzo's team survived a 59–52 win over Northern Iowa. That put MSU up against No. 6 Tennessee, which had upset Ohio State before falling to the Spartans, 70–69.

The second Final Four game pitted West Virginia, which had ousted No. 1 Kentucky in the East Regional, 73–66, against Duke, a 78–71 victor over Baylor in the South Regional. Duke eliminated Purdue 70–57 in the first game of the Sweet Sixteen.

The Butler-MSU contest was a battle worthy of its stage before Butler persevered 52–50. The Spartans opened with a 6–0 run, but Hayward tied it with a pair of three-pointers.

Butler's offense was stagnant at times, but the Bulldogs' defensive work also stymied the Spartans. Hayward and Mack combined for 25 of Butler's first 28 points.

After Howard picked up two quick fouls, MSU enjoyed an eleven-point lead. With Jukes and Smith doing yeoman work in relief of Howard, the Dawgs were tied at halftime and led 38–33 five minutes into the second period. Veasley's steal and layup put Butler ahead 44–37 at 12:15.

The game turned around on a spectacular play by the Bulldogs' Vanzant with ninety seconds to play in regulation. Hayward misfired on a jumper from the left corner, but as the ball left the end of the court, Vanzant leaped behind the basket and fired it back to a driving Hayward for a basket that put Butler up 50–46. The Spartans cut it to 50–47 on a free throw by Darrell

Summers and got within 50–49 when Draymond Green converted two more foul shots into a one-point game. Nored missed a jumper at 0:30 seconds but made two free ones with 0:06 on the clock. Michigan State's Konie Lucious missed the first of two free throws with two seconds remaining and Hayward rebounded the missed second free throw for the clincher.

Hayward led the Bulldogs with 19 points and 9 rebounds.

13 | FOR CRONE, THERE'S NO PLACE LIKE HOME

BRANDON CRONE WAS ABLE TO follow the fortunes of the Butler Bulldogs from half a world away in 2010, but when his alma mater reached the Final Four, there was nothing like being there in person.

Crone, a starting forward for the Bulldogs from 2004 through 2007, was playing professional basketball overseas during March Madness that year. While he didn't want his pro team to lose, he admittedly had mixed feelings.

"We were in the playoffs and we were down two games to one. If we lost then, the series was over and the Final Four was the next weekend," he recalled. "I had about two days that I could try to make it. I didn't try to throw the game at all. We went for the win and we got beat."

Crone, a native of Frankfort, Indiana, went to his coach and asked for help in making a quick trip home. Normally, the pro teams pick up travel costs, but in this case Crone had to help with the airfare. "But I was able to fly back and A. J. [Graves] and Brian [Ligon] and I all watched together. I made it back just in time. To be there, that was special."

Crone, now a member of Butler's basketball staff, said the entire weekend was surreal.

"No question. I went to the open practice and there were thirty thousand people there. That gave me goose bumps," Crone said. "I thought if we could just have gotten past Florida in 2007 that could have been us. That was their closest game. They beat almost everybody by like 20 points. There were a couple of bad calls down the stretch."

14 | "PLUMP DOESN'T NEED A STUNT DOUBLE—EXACTLY"

CBS SPORTS, WHICH TELEVISED THE 2010 Final Four from Lucas Oil Fieldhouse, came up with a gimmick designed to display the short distance between the Butler campus and the site of the games. Throughout the week, Butler's surprising run to the championship games had been compared with Hickory's mythical run to the Indiana high school championship in the 1986 movie *Hoosiers.*

The movie was based on former Butler star Bobby Plump's game-winning basket for Milan in the 1954 state finals. CBS enticed Plump to demonstrate the distance by allegedly dribbling a basketball from Hinkle Fieldhouse to the site of the 2010 Final Four.

That's a distance of about eight miles for a man in his 70s to walk while dribbling, but don't believe everything you see on television.

"They asked me to start at the fieldhouse and dribble down to Lucas Oil," Plump said. "I dribbled across the court and got to the end of the parking lot. Then, we got in a car and we stopped at four or five different places to dribble again. The guy had listed the number of steps and we'd drive some more and then get out and dribble some more. I didn't dribble all the way, but it was as if I had."[1]

15 | A DAVID-AND-GOLIATH STORY

A STUNNED BASKETBALL WORLD WATCHED Butler play for the national championship on April 5, 2010. Almost everybody assumed the small school on Indy's north side had little chance against the big, bad Blue Devils from Durham, North Carolina.

Duke was the perennial strongboy of college basketball, annually recruiting McDonald's All-Americans and coached to the limit by Mike Krzyzewski. Duke had its own corps of loyal supporters but may have been disliked by more fans than any other team. Butler, the sentimental favorite, would receive most of the fan support in the Monday night game.

Butler president Bobby Fong addressed a pep rally on campus before the game and noted messages of support from a soldier in Iraq and other fans as far-flung as New Zealand, Europe, and a cruise ship at sea. Butler's journey to this special night is recapped in Table 15.1.

Duke's road to the title game started with a 73–44 win over Arkansas-Pine Bluff and continued with a 68–53 victory over California. The Blue Devils eliminated Purdue, 70–57, and then beat third-seeded Baylor, 78–71. After Butler edged Michigan State, Duke established itself as the tournament favorite by blitzing West Virginia, 78–57. Butler was collecting sympathy going into Monday night.

Interviewed before a nationwide audience, Krzyzewski said Butler's defense concerned him the most.[1] The Bulldogs kept everything as normal as possible between games, even going to class on Monday morning. The *New York Times* called it the "most eagerly awaited championship game in years."[2]

With 70,930 fans packed into Lucas Oil Stadium, the Bulldogs took the court to the strains of the *Butler War Song*, supported by their mascot, Blue II, and most of the people in attendance. At an hour when many kids are in bed, the orange basketball—the color first suggested by Hinkle—was tossed up between Brian Zoubek and Matt Howard.

Butler missed seven of its first eight shots but stayed close by outrebounding the stronger Blue Devils. Foul trouble curtailed Howard's time in the first half, but Jukes picked up the slack by scoring 10 points as the Dawgs stayed within 33–32 at halftime.

Mack and Hahn put Butler ahead 12–11 with three-pointers, and Hayward went coast-to-coast for a spinning inside bucket, but Duke forged a 26–20 lead at 5:10 before halftime. Jukes then made four more baskets to close down the period.

The Bulldogs were looking at minor deficits for most of the second half. Two foul shots by Jon Scheyer gave the Dukies a 56–51 lead, but Howard and Hayward each made two free throws to cut the lead to a point. With 3:15 left, Duke again was up by five, 60–55.

Howard, who only played nineteen minutes in the game, scored at 1:40 and again at 1:55, leaving the Bulldogs a point behind. Butler regained the ball with 37 seconds to play and retained possession after a deflection out of bounds at 13.6 seconds.

The pass came in to Hayward, who drove right of the lane and arched a soft jumper while falling away from the lengthy Zoubek. The shot was perfectly straight but came off the back rim into Zoubek's hands prior to a Mack foul at 3.6 seconds.

The situation looked hopeless for the Bulldogs, who didn't see things that way. Zoubek intentionally missed the second of two free throws and Hayward rebounded. The six-foot-eight sophomore quickly covered the backcourt, and as Howard leveled Kyle Singler with a crushing pick, Hayward fired a shot—seemingly with little desperation—that bounced off the back of the rim, leaving Duke ahead 61–59.

Six inches shorter and Butler would not only have been national champion, but the game would probably have been remembered as the best in college basketball history.

It may have been anyway.

Table 15.1 Butler's Record in 2009–10

Date	Opponent	Score
Nov. 14	Davidson	W, 73–62
Nov. 18	@ Northwestern	W, 67–54
Nov. 21	@ Evansville	W, 64–60
Nov. 26	Minnesota, 76 Classic in Anaheim, CA	L, 73–82
Nov. 27	UCLA, 76 Classic in Anaheim, CA	W, 69–67
Nov. 29	Clemson, 76 Classic in Anaheim, CA	L, 69–70
Dec. 2	@ Ball State	W, 59–38
Dec. 5	Valparaiso	W, 84–67
Dec. 8	Georgetown, Jimmy V Classic in New York, NY	L, 65–72
Dec. 12	Ohio State	W, 74–66
Dec. 19	Xavier	W, 69–68
Dec. 22	@ UAB	L, 57–67
Dec. 31	Wisconsin-Green Bay	W, 72–49
Jan. 2	Wisconsin-Milwaukee	W, 80–67
Jan. 8	@ Wright State	W, 77–65
Jan. 10	@ Detroit Mercy	W, 64–62
Jan. 14	Cleveland State	W, 64–55
Jan. 16	Youngstown State	W, 91–61
Jan. 21	@ Loyola (IL)	W, 48–47
Jan. 23	@ Illinois-Chicago	W, 84–55
Jan. 29	@ Wisconsin-Green Bay	W, 75–57
Jan. 31	@ Wisconsin-Milwaukee	W, 73–66
Feb. 4	Detroit Mercy	W, 63–58
Feb. 6	Wright State	W, 74–62
Feb. 8	Loyola (IL)	W, 62–47
Feb. 11	@ Youngstown State	W, 68–57
Feb. 13	@ Cleveland State	W, 70–59
Feb. 17	Illinois-Chicago	W, 73–55
Feb. 20	Siena, BracketBuster	W, 70–53
Feb. 26	@ Valparaiso	W, 74–69
March 6	Wisconsin-Milwaukee	W, 68–59
March 9	Wright State	W, 70–45
March 18	UTEP, NCAA in San Jose, CA	W, 77–59
March 20	Murray State, NCAA in San Jose, CA	W, 54–52
March 25	Syracuse, NCAA in Salt Lake City, UT	W, 63–59
March 27	Kansas State, NCAA in Salt Lake City, UT	W, 63–56
April 3	Michigan State, Final Four in Indianapolis	W, 52–50
April 5	Duke, Final Four in Indianapolis	L, 59–61

Source. Data compiled by author.

16 | COMING DOWN OFF THE MOUNTAIN

BUTLER UNIVERSITY WOULD NEVER BE the same. With the end of the 2009–10 season and its 103 days without a loss, Butler and its fans had lived through a winter wonderland. Long forgotten were the 44 days without a victory experienced by Collier's first team.

Indianapolis department stores that in the past had only sold school gear supporting Indiana, Purdue, and Notre Dame now found a market for Butler sweatshirts. A Butler fan visiting in Connecticut struck up a conversation with another man also wearing Butler blue. Butler's admissions office received mailbags of applications. People who hadn't known what state Butler was in were googling the university on their computers. The Bulldogs were receiving heroes' applause at public appearances. Blue II could hardly keep up with the demands of his newfound popularity.

The Butler fan base, growing like a July cornfield, was already looking ahead to next year. Stevens would have to replace Veasley—assuming Butler didn't have to replace Stevens himself—but as the days passed, a new concern entered the conversation: Would Hayward turn professional early?

It seemed so unlikely at first. Butler athletes had always hung around as long as a four-year student loan. But Hayward, the baby-faced assassin, the kid with the aw' shucks demeanor and the seventh-grade haircut, was almost too good for the program.

Stevens and Gordon's parents, Jody and Gordon Sr., tried to get a feeling for his worth to NBA teams and concluded that he would be a top 20 selection. On April 14, 2010, it was announced that he would submit his name for consideration but not hire an agent, which would have automatically ended his college career. As the May 8 deadline approached, Gordon Jr. announced that he would continue with his plan to turn professional. The Utah Jazz made him the ninth overall pick in the draft on June 24.

Some Utah fans voiced displeasure at the selection, possibly thinking Hayward needed to develop physically. After a modest first season in which he averaged 5.4 points a game, Gordon improved his statistics each of the next six seasons until scoring 22 points a game in 2016–17 and being named to the NBA All-Star team.

As good as his scoring, rebounding, and assists have been, Utah coach Quin Snyder claims Hayward's biggest contribution to the Jazz was his defense.

With Hayward gone, all the pundits were ready to count Butler out of the national spotlight. Critics assumed Butler was a onetime wonder and shoved it out of their mindset. By losing Hayward, the Bulldogs had lost the straw that stirred the drink, except that Stevens wasn't out of straws. He still had Mack, Howard, and Nored. Stepping into the void were Shawn Vanzant, Chase Stigall, Andrew Smith, Khyle Marshall, Erik Fromm, and Garrett Butcher. Most of all, there was still Stevens himself, who had passed up other jobs to remain at Butler.

Chris Holtmann, then the coach at Gardner-Webb, said Butler's tournament run was no fluke.

Butler's Final Four teams were outstanding on defense and played a very physical game. Perhaps the Bulldogs' success contributed to more schools playing in the same manner?

"It might have, but those teams were very athletic," Holtmann said. "The 2010 team was as talented as any team in the country. They had great personnel, an outstanding coaching staff, and an elite head coach. It's not a shock that they went head to head with Duke. If they'd played that game ten times, they'd probably beat them at least four or five. They were just an elite team. The 2011 team that lost to Connecticut was still very good defensively. They got hot really late and they did a great job."[1]

It looked like the party was over one month into the 2010–11 season.

Butler opened Louisville's new arena in its second game and took a 15-point beating from the perennial power. Another loss was a made-for-television rematch between Butler and Duke in East Rutherford, New Jersey. Late in the season the Dawgs lost consecutive conference games to Milwaukee, Valparaiso, and Youngstown State.

Stuck with a 14–9 record, the Bulldogs simply won their next fourteen games, making them an ever bigger surprise in 2011 than they had been in 2010. As one wag said, "We wondered who this year's Butler would be. It turned out to be Butler."

Butler made the field for the 2011 NCAA Tournament as the No. 8 seed, named to face No. 9 Old Dominion in its opening game in Washington, DC. The eighth seed is one of the least desirable because, by nature, the Nos. 8 and 9 are evenly matched. But, also, if the No. 8 seed wins, it has always played the region's No. 1 seed in its second game.

Nonetheless, Butler would beat Old Dominion and top-seeded Pittsburgh in two incredible finishes. Howard avoided a first-round loss by the Bulldogs with a last-second follow-up shot that beat Old Dominion 60–58 in a Southeast Regional game. Paired now against No. 1 Pittsburgh, the Dawgs rode a 30-point performance by Mack to a 71–70 victory.

Butler trailed 69–68 with 7.1 seconds to play and had the ball out of bounds under its own basket. Mack inbounded it to Vanzant at the top of the lane, and Shawn drove toward the bucket before slipping a pass to Smith, who scored to put the Bulldogs ahead 70–69 with 1.4 seconds to play. Pittsburgh rolled the ball toward midcourt, and Mack raced the Panthers in an attempt to intercept it. Instead, he fouled Pitt's Gilbert Brown with 1.4 ticks on the clock.

Brown, a 79 percent foul shooter, made the first and missed the second. Howard rebounded and tried to heave a ninety-four-foot desperation shot to the other end of the court. With less than a second remaining, he was whacked across the arms and awarded two free throws. Matt made the first, intentionally missed the second, and helped Butler escape with the one-point win.

Having knocked off the No. 1 seed in the Southeast Regional, the Bulldogs moved on to a Sweet Sixteen date in New Orleans against fourth-seeded Wisconsin, which brought a 23–8 record out of the Big Ten. The Badgers had advanced by beating Belmont 72–58 and Kansas State 70–65. Butler jumped on them early and held off a second-half rally for a 61–54 victory.

Butler and Wisconsin were similar teams, both strong on defense with few turnovers and strong foul shooting. Wisconsin managed a 5–1 lead before the Bulldogs turned up the intensity and took a 33–24 halftime lead. Vanzant scored successive baskets, and his subsequent steal gave the Dawgs an 18–11 lead. Howard's second three-pointer of the first half gave Butler its nine-point margin.

Wisconsin's press gave the Bulldogs some headaches in the second half, forcing them into an uncommon 13 turnovers, but except for 22 points by All-Big Ten guard Jordan Taylor, the Badgers were held in check. Another Wisconsin star, center Jon

Leuer, made only 1 of 12 shots. Meanwhile, the Bulldogs got 20 points and 12 rebounds from Howard and 13 points from Mack.

The victory thrust Butler into the Elite Eight for the second time in its history and set up a match against second-seeded Florida, which had previously eliminated Santa Barbara 79–51, UCLA 73–65, and Brigham Young 83–74.

17 | BULLDOGS ARE IN THE FINAL FOUR AGAIN

THE ELITE EIGHT BATTLE IN 2011 matched two brilliant young coaches who would later meet again in the NBA: Brad Stevens and Billy Donovan. It would require forty-five minutes of intense basketball by two hungry teams before Butler would post a 74–71 victory over Florida.

Each team had lost eight times going into the game, but Butler advanced to the Final Four in Houston by excelling in a couple of categories. First, the Dawgs pulled down 16 offensive rebounds, twice as many as the Southeastern Conference team, and they also had a 41–34 rebounding edge over the second-seeded Gators. Second, Mack scored a game-high 27 points, making 8 of 20 shots.

One Bulldog who was especially looking forward to the game was freshman Khyle Marshall, a Florida native who hadn't been recruited by his home state university. Marshall was especially strong on the offensive board, and he damaged the Gators with 7 offensive rebounds and 10 points in twenty-one minutes of play.

Mack's 14 points kept Butler within 33–32 at halftime after Florida moved 10 points ahead with seven minutes remaining. Center Vernon Macklin made 7 of his 10 shots, and the No. 2

seed shot 48 percent while excelling from the paint. Butler went eight minutes with only one field goal.

However, left-handed marksman Hahn hit a key three-pointer that cut into the ten-point deficit, and after Mack made two foul shots, Hahn drilled another three. Butler closed within a basket when Howard slipped a scoring pass inside to Marshall. Smith blocked successive shots after Florida extended its lead to 31–27, and Marshall's follow-up made it 33–32 at the half.

Smith pulled down 8 rebounds before halftime and Marshall added 8. Butler fans had a scare when Mack went down with an ankle injury late in the period.

The second half and overtime of Butler's 74–71 victory was one of the hardest fought in school history. The Bulldogs couldn't stop Macklin, and Florida was ahead 47–40 eight minutes into the second half. Florida's lead reached 9 before Stevens played a hunch and sent freshman Chrishawn Hopkins into the game. The former Manual High star hit a quick three to return fire to the Dawgs' bellies. Vanzant's three closed it to 57–52, and Butler tied it at 57 on Mack's coast-to-coast drive. It was tied at 60 when overtime beckoned.

Perhaps the most important play of the game occurred when Marshall followed a missed shot with a Herculean effort leading to a three-point play that gave Butler a 65–62 lead. The freshman lay prone pumping his fist in delight.

The Gators last led at 70–69, whereupon Mack hit his fourth three of the game. Shelvin's two foul shots at 10.6 seconds ended the scoring, and Butler had stunned the basketball world again.

18 | A NEW ROLE FOR THE DAWGS

BUTLER HAD BASICALLY BEEN THE underdog for most of the past two tournaments, but as the 2011 Final Four arrived, the Bulldogs were in the unusual role of favorite. For only the second tournament game since the previous March, Butler would wear their white home uniforms in the tournament, marking the higher seed in the upcoming game.

Virginia Commonwealth, or VCU as the Richmond, Virginia, school apparently preferred, was now the Cinderella team. Coached by the colorful Shaka Smart, VCU was like Butler in that none of the pundits considered its advancement a fluke. The Rams were going to have a lot of fan support that had previously been going to the Bulldogs. Nonetheless, Butler pulled out a 70–62 victory.

While Butler came out of the Southeast Regional as its No. 8 seed, VCU was the No. 11 seed out of the Southwest. An at-large team from the Atlantic-10 (A-10) Conference, and an eleven-time loser during the regular season, the Rams were among the so-called First Four who needed to win a qualifying game in Dayton, Ohio, to make the second round. VCU advanced by beating Southern California 59–46.

The Rams then defeated sixth-seeded Georgetown 74–56 in Chicago before pounding sixth-seeded Purdue 94–76 for a trip to the Sweet Sixteen. VCU pulled a minor upset by toppling No. 10 Florida State 72–71 in overtime and reached Houston by upsetting No. 1 seeded Kansas 71–61. Both Butler and Virginia Commonwealth had taken out No. 1 seeds. The Rams' biggest threat was Jamie Skeen, who had 26 points and 10 rebounds against Kansas.

After Butler scored the first 5 points, VCU tallied 11 straight and used its quickness to build a 15–7 lead at 13:12 of the first half. Butler responded by scoring the next 8 to tie it. Nine offensive rebounds, including three each by Howard and Marshall, turned the game around and helped Butler to a 34–28 halftime lead. The Bulldogs shot only 33 percent but made 13 of 15 foul shots. Mack's 13 first-half points included 4 of 5 from the field.

The Rams regained the lead early in the second period despite Hahn making a pair of three-pointers among his 8 straight Butler points. Midway through the second half, the Dawgs gained a seven-point lead and never trailed again, pushing their advantage to 11 in the final minute. Butler dominated the backboards 48–32 and grabbed 16 off its own board, including 5 by Marshall. Skeen's 27 points helped keep VCU in the game. VCU's final record for the season was 28–12.

Mack hit 8 of his 11 shots and scored 24.

19 | SOME DAYS SHOTS WON'T FALL

AS EVENING ROLLED AROUND ON April 4, 2011, the Butler Bulldogs were no longer a Cinderella team. They had played smash mouth with both Florida and VCU, and for the second year in a row, they were forty minutes from a national title. They had the most experienced players in the tournament, not to mention the toughest. Winning an NCAA championship no longer seemed improbable.

Connecticut was a formidable opponent, but the Huskies had dropped nine games during the season while finishing ninth in the Big East. UConn needed to win five games in five days to win the conference tournament and make the NCAA field. UConn had two national titles but had already played ten games in the previous four weeks.

Butler's return to the final game without Hayward stunned the experts, but the Bulldogs were beginning to make believers of the common fans. Both teams had dodged several bullets along the way: Butler barely escaped Old Dominion, Pittsburgh, and Florida; UConn beat Kentucky 56–55 in the national semifinal after edging Arizona 65–63 to reach the Final Four.

What might have been Butler's finest hour turned out to be its worst nightmare. The Bulldogs played hard. They played almost error free. They played passionate defense. They played with a lid on the basket.

In the opening moments, Mack missed a couple of layups that were to be a sign of things to come. Mack, who had made 8 of 11 in the previous game, would go 4 of 15 in the championship contest. He had open shot after open shot but few of them went in. Teammate Howard, who along with Mack had made one clutch play after another throughout the tournament, missed 12 of his 13 shots, many of them from close to the basket.

A shot chart for the first half showed the Bulldogs taking 6 shots within six feet and missing them all.

Yet, somehow Butler led at halftime 22–19 despite making only 22 percent of its 27 shots.

"Inexplicable," said CBS announcer Clark Kellogg at one point during the game.

"The worst half of basketball I've ever seen in a national championship game," said his coworker, Greg Anthony.

The second half was worse—they hit but 1 of 13 from within the three-point arc for a paltry shooting percentage of 16.1 percent.

Stigall opened the second half with a three-pointer that gave Butler a 25–19 lead. However, the time was 12:35 when Vanzant scored Butler's next field goal. At that point, UConn owned a 33–28 edge that would expand to 14 points with five minutes to play.

The Bulldogs claimed 20 offensive rebounds but were still outrebounded 53–41. They committed only six turnovers and limited UConn All-American Kemba Walker to 5 of 19 shots. Still, the bitter aftertaste for the Bulldogs was the fact that if they had made a fourth of their shots, they would have been national champions. Unfortunately, 18.8 percent wasn't good enough.

20 | ALL IN THE FAMILY

SHAWN VANZANT TRAVERSED AN EXTREMELY rocky road to get to Butler.[1] His mother died of cancer at age 39, leaving her 2-year-old son with a father who was a diabetic. Later, his father became unable to take care of Shawn and his older brother, who had gotten into trouble with the law. Yet, Vanzant found love in a new family that took him in as one of their own.

Vanzant was a standout player at Wharton High in Tampa, Florida, when his coach, Tommy Tonelli, became aware of his star player's situation. Vanzant felt his only option was to move in with his grandmother in Cleveland, Ohio, which would have required leaving his team. Vanzant wanted to stay in Tampa, so he approached his coach about the problem.

Tonelli relayed Shawn's plight to the mother of one of Vanzant's teammates. Lisa Litton agreed, on a temporary basis, to take Shawn into her home, where he joined her husband, Jeff, and their three sons. Litton could relate to Vanzant's problems. Litton's own mother had walked out on her family when Lisa was six, and she never heard from her again. Soon Lisa and her family unofficially adopted Shawn. Then, that initial invitation to spend a few nights at their home evolved into a major commitment when Vanzant's father signed guardianship papers over to the Littons.

The fact that Vanzant is African American and the Littons are Caucasians didn't matter to them. Not surprisingly, people would appear startled when Lisa identified Shawn as her son. When she asked Shawn how she should react, she said he replied, "If I say you're my mom, that should be good enough."[2]

When it came time to choose a college, Butler became the only school Vanzant seriously considered. He slowly matured with the Bulldogs and as a senior was a major reason Butler reached the Final Four for the second straight year.

21 | MACK FOLLOWS HAYWARD TO THE NBA

FOR THE SECOND STRAIGHT YEAR, Stevens faced a problem never encountered by a Butler team before. His best player, although retaining eligibility, was going to turn pro ahead of schedule. Mack, a guiding force on both trips to the national championship games, would never have a higher rating than at that time. His shooting, toughness, and leadership would make him thirty-fourth overall pick of the Washington Wizards in the 2011 NBA draft.

Shelvin's tour of duty with the Wizards was short. The NBA lockout saw him join his new team on December 9, but his best game was a 12-point outing against Orlando in February. The following July he joined the Wizards' summer league, and in October the Wizards waived him. He split the 2012–13 season with the Philadelphia 76ers and Maine of the NBA Development League.

Mack gained some stability in 2014 when he signed a three-year contract with the Atlanta Hawks for $7.3 million, according to basketballinsider.com. In 2016 he joined former teammate Hayward when he was traded to Utah.

Meanwhile, Stevens took on the challenge of coaching a team without a superstar. Butler's 22–15 record in 2011–12 failed to get the Dawgs into the NCAA Tournament, but they won two games in the College Basketball Invitational before dropping an overtime game to Pittsburgh. Stevens built around Smith, Nored, Marshall, Stigall, and newcomers Roosevelt Jones, Erik Fromm, Kameron Woods, Alex Barlow, and Jackson Aldridge.

That season would be Butler's last in the Horizon League, and it would drop the championship game of the conference tournament to Valparaiso, 65–46.

22 | LOOKING PAST THE HORIZON

BUTLER EXPERIENCED ITS GREATEST BASKETBALL success while a member of the Horizon League, which rode Butler's coattails to its own success. The conference's statistics were boosted significantly when the Bulldogs reached the NCAA Tournament's final game in 2010 and 2011. On one occasion, a Horizon League school posted "Thanks Butler" on its electric scoreboard when the Bulldogs played there.

The Horizon League, headquartered in Indianapolis, sent twenty-four teams to the NCAA Tournament between 1995 and 2011, and on five occasions those teams made the Sweet Sixteen. Butler carried the brunt of the league's success, reaching the Sweet Sixteen in 2003, 2007, 2010, and 2011.

Butler was a member of the Horizon League, originally named the Midwestern City Conference (MCC), between 1979 and 2012. The league name was changed to Horizon in 2001. The MCC was granted an automatic bid to the NCAA Tournament in 1981, but Butler went from 1962 until 1997 without making the field. The league was only guaranteed one berth, and winning the season-ending conference tournament was usually the only path into the event.

Even if the Bulldogs won the regular-season championship, they usually had to withstand the challenge of conference tournament play, and Butler always had a target on its back. Wright State, Cleveland State, and Green Bay, among others, could be tough matchups with a lot on the line.

When Butler didn't win the Horizon tournament, it was hard for it to beat enough highly rated teams to make it to the NCAA Big Dance.

"I'm not sure we faced a ranked team in the seven years of playing in the Horizon League," Collier said.

Butler's two trips to the Final Four gave the school a chance to shake the mid-major level and get into a tougher league. In 2012–13 Butler was admitted to the Atlantic-10, a definite step up in competition. In their only season in the A-10, the Bulldogs posted a 27–9 record, including a win over top-ranked Indiana, but lost to Marquette in the second round of the national championship.

23 | JONES IS ONE OF A KIND

ROOSEVELT JONES MAY HAVE BEEN the most unique player ever to wear a Butler uniform. He also may have been one of the best ever to play for the Bulldogs.

At six feet four and 230 pounds, Jones looked more like a linebacker than a basketball player. He could score baskets from every angle but couldn't, or wouldn't, shoot a jump shot. He wasn't a good foul shooter either, but he usually made them in the clutch. He was only a modest jumper, but he once blocked four shots in one game. Sometimes he seemed to be launching shots with his elbow, but they often went in.

He missed an entire season with an injury, and it was no coincidence that Butler lost seventeen games that year. Nor was it coincidental that the Bulldogs won forty-five games over the two seasons after he returned.

Purdue coach Matt Painter probably provided the most apt description of Jones. "He can't shoot! Period! He can't shoot, and he's a great player," Painter said after Jones had orchestrated a win over the Boilermakers with 19 points, 11 rebounds, and 5 assists.[1]

"So many guards that are players want to be something they're not. They're looking at other players and say, 'I wish I could be like him.' It would drive 99 percent of all college guards that play this game crazy that they couldn't shoot, and he's good with it. He just wants Butler to win," Painter said.

Jones didn't have a three-point shot in his arsenal, attempting only one during his first three-and-a-half seasons as a Bulldog. When he finally made one at Marquette, it was a sixty-five-foot heave at the end of a half.

"He's not only unique in his skill set," Holtmann said, "he's also unique because there aren't many people who have his competitive drive. That makes him unique. His competitive greatness in the critical moments in games make him unique because it's a special quality."

Jones came out of O'Fallon, Illinois, in 2011. For a kid who couldn't shoot, he hit 6l percent in high school and set an O'Fallon record with 240 steals.

Jones was a freshman at Butler the year after its second trip to the Final Four, and Nored was the only starter returning from the 2010 team. The Bulldogs struggled to a 22–15 record and missed the NCAA Tournament. Jones averaged 8 points on the season, and the Dawgs were beaten by Valparaiso in the Horizon League Tournament, 65–46.

With Butler moving to the A-10 in 2012–13, Roosevelt was named conference Player of the Week three times and contributed 16 points, 12 rebounds, and 7 assists as Butler upset No. 1 Indiana. Jones's most spectacular moment came at home in a nationally televised game against No. 8 Gonzaga.

The Bulldogs trailed by a point when guard Alex Barlow was called for steps with only seconds remaining. The Zags took the ball out near midcourt, but the inbounds pass by David Stockton was stolen by Jones, who slipped through traffic and launched a teardrop over seven-foot Kelly Olynyk to seal the win for the Bulldogs, 64–63.

The game was played in a festive atmosphere provided when ESPN staged a pregame celebration that attracted a large crowd of Butler students in the morning and was followed by a classic game that featured thirteen lead changes. Jones led the Dawgs with 20 points and made 7 of 10 shots. Gonzaga's star Olynyk had 24 points and would later play for Stevens with the Boston Celtics.

Butler trailed 63–62 when Barlow was called for traveling with three seconds to play. Jones's steal and quick basket saved the day as students rushed the court.

The Bulldogs were preparing to play in their third conference in three years when two major developments occurred. In July 2013 Stevens accepted the job as head coach of the Celtics. Then, in early August, the Dawgs learned that Jones would miss the entire Big East season—Butler's first in that conference—with a wrist injury suffered during the team's trip to Australia. Roosevelt had fallen on his left wrist in a game and damaged a ligament, requiring season-ending surgery.

It was a devastating injury for new head coach Brandon Miller because Jones was not only the team's top returning scorer and rebounder but also a team leader. When he returned for his junior and senior years, he became an All-Conference player and one of the most talked about players in the Big East. Both he and teammate Kellen Dunham were recruited to play in the Horizon League yet excelled in a conference rated two notches higher. Jones made a school record 134 career starts, ranked eleventh among all Bulldogs with 1,533 points, fifth in career rebounds (814), and eighth in steals (147). Most importantly, the Bulldogs had a 94–46 record with him on the floor.

Jones spent the 2016–17 season with Canton in the NBA Development League.

24 | CLARKE'S STAY IS BRIEF, BUT BRILLIANT

A YEAR AFTER BUTLER MADE its second successive trip to the Final Four, the Bulldogs were having trouble scoring points. Hayward and Mack were in the NBA, and their replacements were still a work in progress. Stevens looked down his bench, which only compounded his frustrations.

Sitting beside him in civilian clothes was perhaps the best collegiate shooter in America, but Rotnei Clarke wasn't eligible until the following season.

However, Clarke was worth the wait.

The Oklahoma native would play only one year in the state of Indiana, but he was the prototypical Hoosier basketball player, a six-foot young man with a magic touch, a quick release, and newspaper clippings of which legends are made. Dissatisfied with the changing coaching situation at the University of Arkansas, Clarke was attracted to the aura that had surrounded Butler in its two runs to the Final Four.[1]

A native of Verdigris, Oklahoma, Clarke was that state's all-time scoring leader with 3,758 points. He scored 30 or more points an astonishing seventy-two times and on entering his sophomore year with the Razorbacks was named the nation's top shooter by Foxsports.com. He scored 51 points against Alcorn State as a sophomore, while making 15 of 21 shots and 13 of 17 three-pointers. As a junior he scored 35 against Vanderbilt and 26 against Kentucky.

Clarke liked Butler but would have to sit out a transfer season in order to play one year for the Bulldogs. He had a spectacular start with his new school, launching an off-balance, last-second heave to beat Marquette in Hawaii. He led the Bulldogs to their first victory ever over a No. 1 team when they upset Indiana in Indianapolis.

He was also injured in one of the scariest mishaps in school history when, after a steal, he was knocked into the basket support in a game at Dayton. While on the floor amid fears of a paralyzing neck injury, Clarke displayed his moxie by saying, "I'm not coming out." Wiser heads prevailed, and it was eight minutes before he was removed and taken to Miami Valley Hospital where it was determined that there was no fracture.

"That was definitely scary. He obviously was a guy we couldn't afford to lose," McGrath said. At the time the Bulldogs were ninth in the poll and played without Clarke for three games, which included an upset loss to LaSalle.

The injury occurred January 12, 2013, during Butler's only season in the A-10. Butler's postseason success helped the Bulldogs land Clarke because his Arkansas team hadn't reached the NCAA Tournament.

Up to fifty colleges reportedly recruited Clarke out of high school, one of which was Butler.

"I wasn't interested in things like top-notch facilities anymore. I was interested in being around good teammates, good people," he told Kelli Anderson of *Sports Illustrated*.[2] Clarke, who was named after former Oklahoma running back Rotnei Anderson, said he profited greatly by teammate Nored's defense against him in practice. He also told Anderson that he would practice alone in Hinkle Fieldhouse and not leave until he had made 500 shots.

Clarke averaged 17 points a game for the season and was first in the A-10 in free-throw shooting and three-pointers. Butler defeated Dayton and LaSalle before losing to Saint Louis in the A-10 Tournament. Clarke went to Australia to play professionally and was named MVP in the Australian National Basketball League.

25 | JUST A HOP, SKIP, AND JUMP AWAY

PENDLETON, INDIANA, IS A HANDY place for Butler's basketball coaches to recruit. It's in an adjoining county from the Butler campus, located off an interstate highway.

You'll find it easily because the Indiana State Reformatory is located nearby. Residents of Pendleton follow Butler basketball, especially since their own Kellen Dunham and Sean McDermott became Bulldogs.

Dunham (class of '18) was among the latest in a line of great shooters to play at Butler. McDermott (class of '21), a redshirt freshman during the 2015–16 season, has yet to make his mark but the potential is there. He now is a top reserve. "He reminds me of [former Bulldog] Drew Streicher defensively," McGrath said of McDermott. "He's kind of long and he gets up into you. If he's guarding you, you're having a bad night."

Dunham was recruited by Stevens and played a strong supporting role as a freshman during Butler's only season in the A-10. Most teams try to foul freshmen in clutch situations, but not Dunham because he made 87 percent. He had been even better as a high school senior, making 92 percent.

As a freshman Kellen scored 17 points in Butler's victory over North Carolina in Hawaii.

During his first year at Butler, Kellen averaged 9.5 points a game and hit 57 three-pointers. Perhaps his most critical was a three in the second half of the Bulldogs' upset of No. 1 Indiana.

Dunham's four-year total of 1,946 points ranks third on Butler's all-time list, trailing only Chad Tucker and Darrin Fitzgerald. His consistency is revealed by the fact that his scoring average varied only from 16.2 to 16.5 over his final three seasons.

Coming out of Pendleton Heights High School, Dunham made the 2012 Indiana All-Star team that played Kentucky and led the state in scoring and foul shooting.

Dunham became the first player to commit to Butler after the Bulldogs first reached the national title game in 2010. Part of the reason? Stevens kept making the easy drive to Pendleton to impress him.

26 | BUTLER GOES BIG TIME IN THE BIG EAST

BUTLER HAD BEEN A MEMBER of the A-10 for only one year when the opportunity arose for it to join the Big East Conference. Collier never hesitated to relocate his school in one of the best basketball leagues in the country. On July 1, 2013, barely three years after Butler surged near the top of the public's consciousness, the Indianapolis school was added to the "new" Big East that also accepted the memberships of Xavier and Creighton.

Xavier had been in the A-10 with Butler while Creighton was in the Missouri Valley Conference (MVC). They joined seven Catholic schools already in the Big East: Marquette, DePaul, Seton Hall, Providence, St. John's, Georgetown, and Villanova.

Membership in the conference had been unstable for years due to the tension between big-time football schools and those whose main interest was basketball. By the time Butler joined, the Big East had gone back to its basketball roots. Since being founded in 1979 by Providence coach Dave Gavitt, the Big East had developed some outstanding basketball rivalries with former members Syracuse, Boston College, Pittsburgh, and Connecticut among others.

The challenges of Butler moving into tougher competition left some fans and alumni concerned. First, travel costs to games would increase significantly. The competition for recruits would become more intense. Also, Butler's enrollment of about five thousand is smaller than every conference school but Providence.

The move required Butler to upgrade the quality of its recruits. Two years earlier the Bulldogs were recruiting for Horizon League competition; now they were battling to compete for players in one of the nation's best leagues.

If some Butler alums questioned the wisdom of the move, Collier did not, nor did he have doubts about leaving the Horizon League for the A-10 a year earlier. Whether the two-step progression made the second move easier is subjective.

"We can't predict something that never happened. We'll never know, but the Big East was not an option in 2013 and the A-10 was," Collier said. "There was this continual movement of leagues. It's settled down a significant amount now, but at the time [of] the breakup of the Big East you could see it coming eventually. When they had this football group and this basketball group, you knew that something was going to happen, but you didn't know when."

Collier said Butler's opportunity to go to the A-10 was a result of the school's success in the 2010 and 2011 basketball tournaments. Butler's trips to the national title game made it one of the most popular teams in America, a team with the reputation of being an underdog that had proven it could compete at the highest level. Besides the two Final Fours, the Bulldogs had won the highly contested preseason NIT and the Great Alaska Shootout while doing well in the Maui Invitational.

"Those same accomplishments helped create the opportunity to go to the Big East, along with the continued success in the A-10," Collier said. "That came about fairly quickly. Our plan was not to leave the A-10 and join the Big East, but circumstances changed."

Reflecting on the move one day after Butler had upset No. 1 Villanova in Hinkle Fieldhouse, Collier added, "If the Big East doesn't break apart, then we're not playing the No. 1 team in the nation last night."

Going to a tougher conference not only presents greater challenges but also greater opportunities. For instance, Villanova was the first top-ranked team to play at Hinkle since Indiana in 1953. Butler can't beat a No. 1 team if it doesn't get an opportunity to play one.

While the "old" Big East lost some schools with strong traditions, ratings give little indication that its talent level has fallen off. Midway through the 2017 season, Big East members Villanova, Creighton, Butler, and Xavier all were rated among the nation's twenty best teams. During its last ten years in the Horizon League, Butler cracked the Top 10 in the Associated Press (AP) poll only twice. Despite its twenty-five-game winning streak in 2010, the Dawgs climbed no higher than eleventh.

The Big East gives the Bulldogs a home schedule that has proven exciting for the fans. Most games at Hinkle are sellouts or close to it.

"That's a testament to how far the program has evolved," McGrath said. "When you look at the cost of season tickets now versus then . . . When I started here in the '80s a sellout was unheard of. To fill it you had to bring in ten thousand Indiana fans and a thousand Butler fans. We tried to have the lower level filled and the upper level was always open. There was no demand, but as the program grew it got better, and you can see the results in better seating and a better facility in every way."

In the late 1950s, Coach Hinkle, hoping to come closer to sellouts at what was then a fifteen-thousand-seat arena, lowered season ticket prices to five dollars. Butler students got in free.

Many years ago Butler had visions of fashioning a major football program with the possibility of expanding Butler Bowl into a giant stadium. Those thoughts eventually dissolved, and Collier didn't intend to bypass a chance to build the basketball program.

"No. The sooner the better," he said. "We want to be more successful than we are in all sports, and we think we're getting there. I just love the challenge."

Dismissing the knowledge that some fans thought the Big East was too great a challenge, he said, "There were some doubters. That's the way of the world. Four years into it there are fewer doubters than there were."

While the Big East probably had the reputation of being a stronger league when it included Syracuse, UConn, and the like, the current ten-team setup hasn't taken a back seat to other major conferences.

"Villanova's championship last year [2016] was a major, major accomplishment for the league. Our league is probably better than a number of people would have thought. The league is really strong," Collier said. "There's a tight philosophy that we all share that says we want to be really, really good at basketball."

27 | WORSE THAN A DEATH IN THE FAMILY

JIM MCGRATH AND HIS WIFE were in Paris on a trip to visit their daughter and son-in-law in Germany when Jim got an email from back home informing him of the worst possible news.

Thinking back to that day in 2013, Jim called it "one of the worst days of my life." Stevens was leaving Butler University to coach the Boston Celtics.

"I looked at my wife and she said, 'Did somebody die?' And I said, 'No, it's worse.' I wanted to get on a plane and come right back," said McGrath, Butler's sports publicist at the time.

"And she said, 'No way!'"

For six years Butler fans had lived in fear that their beloved young coach would forsake the school where his reputation had reached such proportions that several collegiate powers had tried to attract him to their campuses. Several times Stevens had said that people were more important than money and opted to stay at Butler.

During his six seasons as Butler's head coach, he had stared down some of America's most treasured coaches: Jim Boeheim of Syracuse, Roy Williams of North Carolina, Bob Knight of Texas Tech, Mike Krzyzewski of Duke, Billy Donovan of Florida, Mark Few of Gonzaga, Tom Izzo of Michigan State, and Bo Ryan of Wisconsin. Except for that classic two-point loss to Duke in 2010, he had beaten all of them.

Despite coaching vacancies such as UCLA and Illinois being dangled before him, Stevens remained loyal to the Bulldogs. But in coaching Butler to two national championship games, a Sweet Sixteen, two rounds of thirty-two, and with a winning percentage of .772, the boyish coach had established himself as the hottest coaching property in America. Almost totally because of him, Butler had risen from mid-major status to a new membership in the prestigious Big East Conference.

Many thought Stevens had lifted himself up by his bootstraps believing his status as a major conference coach would assure his staying at Butler. No one dreamed that the NBA might interest the former guard at DePauw University. Considering the Celtics' winning tradition, Stevens listened to Celtics president Danny Ainge and received an offer he couldn't turn down. His contract called for him to make $22 million over a six-year period.

Realists had to know that Stevens wouldn't stay at Butler forever. Among those was one of his assistants, Terry Johnson. "I knew if the right team came he would leave," said Johnson. "Boston's tradition is like no other. He wasn't turning that down. In Boston nobody expected him to do much, and they got there faster than anybody thought."

The Celtics had won a record seventeen NBA championships but had fallen on hard times when Stevens arrived. He returned them to contention in only two seasons and generally received high praise from both his players and Boston fans.

Stevens has the reputation of being a coach who prepares flawlessly for an opponent. "We know everything we need to about our opponents, all their tendencies are broken down," then Bulldog sophomore Nored told Billy Witz of the *New York Times*.[1]

Stevens is also considered one of the best at devising out-of-bounds plays. In fact, Krzyzewski ordered a missed free throw at the end of the 2010 Butler game because he reportedly feared what kind of closing play Stevens might set up.

Stevens's Butler teams were known for their defense and tough play. In the Bulldogs' six games in the 2010 NCAA Tournament, only Duke score more than 60 points (61).

Collier, who named Stevens to replace Lickliter when the latter went to Iowa, noted Stevens's calm demeanor around his team was no accident.

"The very first game he ever coached he said he was so nervous he was afraid he'd transfer it to the team," Collier said. "But he vowed he'd never show that again, and that was the end of that."

28 | BARLOW'S FLOATER DOOMS HOOSIERS

ALEX BARLOW WAS A TYPICAL Butler guard, a knockoff of many Bulldogs who preceded him.

To summarize Barlow's game, he wasn't tall and he wasn't particularly fast. Except for spot-up three-pointers, he wasn't an especially good shooter. He might be the last player picked in a scrub game at the schoolyard. At five feet eleven, he wasn't a great rebounder, yet he had 10 in a game against LSU.

Still, Barlow became one of the most respected players in the Big East because he played smarter than the rest. And, most importantly, he was a winner. When Butler upset No. 1 Indiana in December 2012, it was Barlow who scored the winning basket, a floater from inside the lane that found the net after multiple bounces on the rim. When the Bulldogs beat favored North Carolina in the Bahamas in December 2014, it was Barlow who outplayed a Tar Heels team loaded with high school All-Americans.

Barlow had enrolled at Butler without a scholarship but with a dream to someday coach basketball. He got a head start on his chosen profession by being a coach on the floor.

Barlow was the glue that held Butler together during the 2014–15 season: In fact, he was named to *Sports Illustrated*'s All-Glue Team. The Ohio native ranked fifth in steals at his school.

Majoring in finance, he was the Big East Scholar-Athlete of the Year as a junior and as a senior, and he was selected as an Academic All-American.

Barlow played at Cincinnati Moeller High School where he hit 9 of 12 shots in one game. He was a standout shortstop on the baseball team and stole 26 bases in 26 attempts as a senior, one year after he batted .532.

Nonetheless, colleges expressed little interest in Barlow, whose only basketball scholarship offer came from Tiffin, a Division II school in northern Ohio. Hoping to coach someday, he wanted to learn from Butler's Brad Stevens.

Barlow's most famous moment came as a sophomore. When his more explosive teammates were covered defensively, he made a soft eight-footer to beat Indiana.

"We were trying to run a play we'd been using most of the game, trying to hit Rotnei [Clarke] or Kellen [Dunham]," Barlow told the *Cincinnati Enquirer*. "They overplayed Clarke and Kellen couldn't shake open, so I knew I was going to have to make a play."[1] Barlow was hemmed in by the taller Hoosiers, so he flipped up an unorthodox shot with 2.5 seconds left in overtime that bounced true.

Barlow recalled his first individual workout at Butler as a frightening moment of truth.

"I thought, 'Holy cow, what am I doing here?' It was horrible. I never played AAU basketball and now you're playing with some of the best athletes around. It was a different game seeing people like Kameron Woods with long arms, people so physically strong like [Roosevelt] Jones and athletic like Khyle Marshall," he said.[2]

29 | IT WASN'T MILLER TIME

THE WINTER OF 2013–14 WAS dismal both outside and inside of Hinkle Fieldhouse. Former Bulldog guard Brandon Miller (2001–3) had been named to replace the departed Stevens. Not even the coaches who replaced Bob Knight at Indiana and Dean Smith at Carolina faced more pressure.

Stevens was thought to be irreplaceable, a boy king who had taken the Bulldogs to two Final Fours and won four Horizon League titles and three conference tournaments. His teams won 77 percent of their games, and he did it all with a calm demeanor and self-assurance that many coaches lack.

Miller, 34 at the time, was not only replacing a youthful icon but was taking the Bulldogs into their first season in the Big East. Butler, less than two years removed from being a mid-major in the Horizon League, had a largely inexperienced roster going against one of the nation's most prestigious conferences. It got worse when Jones, a future All-Big East selection, missed the season with an injury incurred during the off-season.

There was a concern among Butler fans that the Bulldogs might be out of their league, and Holtmann, who had joined the staff as an assistant in 2013, said he worried that the program wasn't as close to the competitive level he had expected when he came to Butler.

"I did worry about that. I also heard a lot of people questioning us that year on why make the move," he said. "I think they thought that was what happened when you move two leagues in two years. They feared playing that kind of competition night in and night out might beat you up."

The injury to Jones was a significant setback to Miller, Holtmann acknowledged, adding, "We had a lot of new faces, a very large freshman class that had signed to play for Brad. It's your first year in a new league that's really good, and then you have these new faces and you're trying to blend new and old. It was a lot for us as coaches, and it was a lot for a first-time head coach.

"We still had some good players. I mean Kellen Dunham, Alex Barlow, Kam Woods, Khyle Marshall. We had some guys that next year, with the addition of Roosevelt Jones and a freshman class, finished second in the Big East."

Butler's roster was thin, and as the season wore on, the Bulldogs' lack of depth on the bench took a toll. Gone from Stevens's last Butler team were Clarke, Smith, and Stigall. Stevens's last recruiting class featured starter Andrew Chrabascz, Elijah Brown, and Nolan Berry. By the following season, Brown and Berry would be gone, and so would be Coach Miller.

Butler started its first season in the Big East with five straight wins, including an overtime victory over Vanderbilt. The Bulldogs dropped successive two-point games to Oklahoma State and LSU in Orlando, Florida, and then won their next five, including a win over Purdue. The Bulldogs' debut in the Big East was a three-point overtime loss to Villanova in Hinkle.

Not a bad start, but disaster lay ahead. Butler lost its next four, one by double overtime and two by one extra period. The Dawgs beat Marquette in overtime but lost ten of their last thirteen games to finish 14–17.

"We got into this deal that teams get into sometimes where you're close and you're close and close again and you can't get over the hump," Holtmann said. "It spiraled to 4–14. It got out of control for us."

Then, in one of the more mysterious coaching changes of its time, Miller asked for a leave of absence for unidentified health reasons on October 1, 2014. A few months later, the university announced that he wouldn't return for the 2014–15 season.

Coaching changes that close to the season opener are not only unusual but often penal for a program. Indiana fired Bob Knight on September 10, 2000, and it took several years for the Hoosiers to approach their once lofty heights. At Butler, Collier again looked to his own staff and named Holtmann to be interim coach. By midseason Holtmann had the job for keeps.

Miller's coaching reputation was exemplary when hired by Butler. He had served as an assistant at Butler and Ohio State before leaving coaching to spend more time with his family. After being away a year, he returned as a special assistant to John Groce at Illinois and, in April 2013, returned to Butler as an assistant under Stevens.

30 | BRAD STEVENS IN DISGUISE?

BY THE TIME HOLTMANN HAD finished his first year as Butler coach, his stature had reached such heights that he was thought to be a Brad Stevens clone. In his third season, Holtmann was named both Big East and National Coach of the Year.

The 43-year-old Holtmann had one advantage over the seven previous successors to Hinkle. None of them had been a head coach in another college, whereas Holtmann had been the head man at Gardner-Webb for three seasons. His final season at the North Carolina school saw his team win twenty-one games, and although his three-year record was a modest 44–54, his teams' progress had drawn praise.

Holtmann had made an unusual move in 2013 by leaving a head job to take an assistant's position under Brandon Miller. Holtmann had known Miller and was pleased to work with the former Butler guard when he took over at Butler. When Miller departed in 2014, Holtmann was named interim coach, and Collier removed his temporary status three months later. Holtmann's players lauded the choice and bought into his system even as Holtmann bought into The Butler Way. Not only did he win forty-five games in his first two seasons at Fairview, but he was only the second Butler coach to make the NCAA Tournament in each of his first two seasons.

His coaching honors after the 2017 season were no surprise because television analysts had been heralding his candidacy all season, and his name was brought up when several coaching vacancies emerged at the end of the season. His national citation came in the form of the John McLendon Award, and he was also among seventeen finalists for the Jim Phelan Coach of the Year Award. The Phelan finalists included such names as Gonzaga's Mark Few, UCLA's Steve Alford, Oregon's Dana Altman, and Kentucky's John Calipari.

A preseason poll picked the Bulldogs as a likely sixth-place finisher in the Big East, which was four spots lower than they ultimately attained.

The Bulldogs' quick reversal from their poor debut in the Big East endeared Holtmann to Butler fans. After tying for seventh in the conference in a preseason poll, the Dawgs went 22–11 during Holtmann's inaugural season and won twelve games in the Big East. They also defeated No. 5 North Carolina 74–66 in the Bahamas.

Butler's disappointing first season in the Big East left many fans worried that their team could not sufficiently recruit for its new league, however. Some players thought to be leaning toward attending Butler backed out when Stevens left. Holtmann's newcomers were Kelan Martin and Tyler Wideman, but their quick development, plus the return of Jones from his injury, boosted the Bulldogs to a second-place finish in the standings. At that point, Holtmann's recruiting abilities took effect.

Butler's depth got better in Chris's next season. Indiana transfer Austin Etherington consistently improved during his second season with the Dawgs, and Saint Bonaventure transfer Jordan Gathers added some more depth. Holtmann's second season saw him win eleven of his first twelve games en route to a 22–11 record.

The Bulldogs went 10–8 in the Big East and lost to Virginia in the second round of the NCAA Tournament that year.

Holtmann is a native of Nicholasville, in central Kentucky, and was a National Association of Intercollegiate Athletics (NAIA) All-American guard at Taylor University in Indiana, where he graduated in 1994. He received his master's degree from Ball State in 2000. In 2009 he was hired by new Ohio University coach John Groce, a former Butler assistant.

Holtmann spent two years on Ohio's staff, helping the Bobcats win the Mid-American Conference (MAC) title and make the NCAA Tournament, where they upset third-seeded Georgetown.

Holtmann said leaving a head coaching job to become an assistant at Butler was the hardest professional decision of his life. "I polled eight of my closest coaching friends and they were split four and four on whether I should do it or not, so I didn't get any help from them," he said. "A couple of them were adamant I should not leave a head coaching job. I had just signed a five-year contract, so why would you do that? I really liked the idea of the move to the Big East. . . . I just felt if we could get good in the Big East with the success I had at Gardner-Webb. . . . We had built it up there quickly and I felt if I came here and we had success maybe I could be a head coach again in a better situation."

Holtmann had known Stevens for about fifteen years. "We got to know each other when he was an assistant here and I was an assistant at Taylor University," he said. "We had talked about working together. I talked about joining his staff on a couple of occasions. It just didn't work out."

Told that many consider him a clone of Stevens, Holtmann said, "I think he's the best; he's proven that. His tenure with the Celtics validates it even more. Brad also has a really great way about how he leads a team and manages a team. Anytime people say I'm similar, I'm reluctant to hear it but certainly appreciative of it because he's great."

31 | CHANGES MAKE A DIFFERENCE: MAKING CHANGES FOR THE BETTER

HOLTMANN KNEW THAT SOME CHANGES were necessary as he entered his first full season as Bulldog coach. He still had a nucleus of good players led by Jones, Dunham, Barlow, Woods, and Chrabascz.

"Our roster needed to change a little bit. There were some young men that weren't quite the Butler fit," Holtmann said. "Some of it took care of itself at the end of the year with a couple of transfers. And then you add Roosevelt Jones. We had a close team that next year. We had a team that was moving in one direction. Sometimes a different place for some young men is better."

The lone player returning as a sophomore was Andrew Chrabascz, a six-foot-seven Rhode Island product who had battled the strongboys of the Big East all his freshman year. All his classmates moved on after that season. "He was great. I'm sure he had it on his mind that his whole class was leaving," Holtmann said. "He played a lot and knew he would continue to play. So why would he leave this when he liked the school and liked the coaches?"

The Bulldogs turned things around and finished the 2014–15 season with a 23–11 slate and won eight of their first nine games. They also beat No. 5 North Carolina and conference rival Georgetown in a holiday tournament. They made the NCAA Tournament but lost an overtime thriller to No. 8 Notre Dame in the second round.

Kameron Woods, a six-foot-nine product from Louisville, was one of Butler's more underrated players during Holtmann's tenure. "Yes, very much so," Holtmann emphasized. "He impacted the game in a lot of ways that didn't show up. He was a tremendous rebounder with a tremendous nose for the ball. He was a unique player. His length provided so many issues for people."

32 | THE CITADEL TAKES A BEATING

IT'S A WONDER BLOOD WASN'T spilled when The Citadel came to Hinkle Fieldhouse for the 2015–16 season opener. Butler's 144–71 victory virtually rewrote the school's record book and had no one crying for a rematch. As Holtmann remarked, "This may be the most unique game ever played."

Butler took a 71–41 halftime lead, then tacked on another 71 points in the second half while shooting 66 percent for the game and 78 percent for the second period. This wasn't a case of a superior team running up the score but of a losing team playing at a pace that guaranteed that would happen. For example, the visitors launched 47 three-point shots in the game, making only 10. There were 60 free throws attempted and 54 fouls whistled against the two teams.

Seven Bulldog players scored in double figures, led by Dunham with 24. Wideman made all 8 of his shots, and Chrabascz hit 6 of 7. The Citadel's trio of P. J. Boutte, Derrick Henry, and Quayson Williams made only 11 of 46 shots, collectively.

Butler hit 56 of 88 shots and blocked 10 attempts by The Citadel, which finished the season with a 10–22 record. The Citadel Bulldogs came in last in the Southern Conference that first year under new coach Robert Franklin "Duggar" Baucom, who had established a reputation for up-tempo play while at VMI.

"I'd known their coach for a while," Holtmann said. "I didn't know it was going to be like that, but I knew it was going to be crazy. We had a couple of our guys say after that game, 'That was fun. Can we do that again tonight?'"

33 | BUTLER REACHES OUT TO BALDWIN

BUTLER'S RECRUITING STRATEGY DOESN'T RULE out blue-chip prospects, the top-of-the-line high school players who often wind up at such basketball factories as Kentucky, Duke, and North Carolina.

"In recruiting there has to be a mutual interest for this thing to work," Holtmann said before taking the head job at Ohio State in June 2017. "We'll spend time on the ones that we feel are mutually interested. We want to recruit the very best players we can recruit. That's our job."

Hayward and Mack were blue-chip players that Butler had snatched away from bigger area schools. Another player with great credentials joined the Bulldogs in 2016–17 after a tiresome recruiting process: Kamar Baldwin, a resident of Winder, Georgia, cracked the starting lineup as a freshman.

Baldwin was called to Butler's attention by a former assistant coach who had moved to another school. "'I don't think we're going to be able to get this young man, but you should take a look,'" Holtmann recalled him saying. "So we went down to take a look at him. [Assistant coach] Emerson Kampen was the first one to go take a look at him. Emerson went down and said, 'Hey, I really like him.'

"Emerson passed him off to [assistant coach] Ryan Pedon, and we made him a huge priority. He knew he was going to have a huge opportunity. He was looking for a basketball school. Our guys did a terrific job recruiting him."

Baldwin excelled in all facets of the game, ranking among the Big East leaders in steals, making shots from all angles, and rebounding despite a six-foot-one frame. His steal from Villanova All-American Josh Hart would help seal Butler's midseason home victory over the defending national champions.

34 | THIRD SEASON IS THE CHARM

WITH CHRABASCZ THE ONLY REMAINING recruit from the Stevens days, Holtmann was ready for a breakout season in 2016–17. It would hit a level seldom reached in school history.

A Big East preseason poll had placed the Dawgs in the middle of the pack, but at that time few had heard of Butler freshman Baldwin. Doubters were prone to consider the loss of Jones and Dunham and underrated the upcoming contributions of transfers Avery Woodson and Kethan Savage and the improvement of center Nate Fowler. By January 4, when Butler made No. 1 Villanova its fourth straight Top 25 victim of the season, the Bulldogs' balloon was soaring.

Riding an extremely difficult schedule, the Bulldogs won their first eight games before stumbling to an inspired Indiana State team in Terre Haute, 72–71. The Bulldogs gave up 12 offensive rebounds and were beaten on the boards, 37–29. Butler's all-time record against the Sycamores had been 70–56.

Otherwise, the Dawgs had some major accomplishments. They beat Northwestern on a last-second shot by the freshman, Baldwin. They beat Vanderbilt 76–66 in a Las Vegas tournament and then whipped No. 8 Arizona 69–65. Coming home, Butler defeated previously unbeaten Utah in Salt Lake City, 68–59.

Everything was pointed toward the Crossroads Classic game against Indiana in Bankers Life Fieldhouse. The Hoosiers were ranked ninth and had beaten two top-three teams, Kansas and North Carolina. After beating Kentucky in the 2016 NCAA Tournament, Hoosier fans were aflame with anticipation.

It was a shootout following in the steps of recent Butler-Indiana games. IU had eight wins wrapped around a stunning loss at Fort Wayne. Butler had ten wins against the one defeat in Terre Haute and took a 42–28 halftime lead against a youthful Hoosier team. Baldwin got IU's attention with 14 points and 5 rebounds. Chrabascz was the floor leader with 14 points and 4 assists, while Martin led the scoring with 28 points.

Still, the Hoosiers closed within a basket in the final minute, and Butler had the ball out of bounds under its own basket. Using a play suggested by Chrabascz, point guard Tyler Lewis slipped an inbounds pass to Tyler Wideman for a clinching dunk.

Butler had beaten archrivals Purdue and IU in successive seasons, and the Dawgs had warmed up for Indiana by also beating No. 22 Cincinnati, 75–65.

Butler's fourth season in the Big East began with a 76–73 upset loss at St. John's, but it rebounded by knocking off Providence at home, 78–61.

35 | DAWGS KNOCK OFF NO. 1 WILDCATS THREE TIMES

VILLANOVA'S WILDCATS HAD WON TWENTY straight games, including fourteen in the 2016–17 season. Butler had slipped up against underdogs Indiana State and St. John's and hadn't beaten Nova in their seven previous meetings. Jay Wright's Wildcats were No. 1 on the heels of an NCAA championship, with the bulk of their starters back, and had defeated previously unbeaten Creighton four days earlier.

Not since 1953 had a top-ranked team played on Butler's home court, that being a 86–57 loss to Indiana. A nationwide television audience tuned in on January 4, 2017, probably expecting another Villanova win.

As it turned out, the Bulldogs had the powerful Wildcats right where they wanted them—in Hinkle Fieldhouse with its raucous 9,206 fans. The same atmosphere prevailed on December 30, 2017, when the Bulldogs beat Nova a third time, 100–93, while shooting 60 percent.

Raising the roof at Hinkle is a monumental feat, but the Butler faithful must have lifted it a few inches in the first when the Dawgs took a six-point lead with 1:46 to play, then kept it aloft even as the visitors twice pulled within four. After sophomore center Nate Fowler extended the margin to the final score of 66–58, hundreds of students rushed the court in celebration.

Winning road games in the Big East Conference is a formidable task; even so, the Bulldogs were due to beat Nova in Indianapolis. In their last three meetings at Hinkle, the Wildcats had triumphed by 3 points in overtime and by 3 and 5 points in regulation, respectively. On those occasions Villanova had been ranked sixth once and eleventh twice.

Butler was ranked eighteenth entering the 2017 game, with voters perhaps showing a lack of respect for a team that had already beaten three Top 25 teams: Arizona, Cincinnati, and Indiana. Apparently, the AP poll reflected voters' disbelief in the Dawgs after the losses at Indiana State and St. John's.

Villanova fans spent the next seven weeks after the January 4 meeting awaiting the rematch in Philadelphia. During that span, the Wildcats lost only once, a 74–72 decision at Marquette on January 24. Nova's only close game leading up to the Butler rematch was a two-point victory over Virginia.

Villanova took to their home court against the Bulldogs full of toughness but found Butler fully prepared for the challenge. Trailing only 29–28 after an intense first half, the Bulldogs shot 60 percent in the second period for a 74–66 victory. Villanova coach Jay Wright said later in a television interview, "Butler could beat anybody. They could win the whole thing."[1]

"More gratifying than beating Villanova in Indianapolis was beating them on their own court," said Butler assistant Ryan Pedon. "Their seniors had never lost a game in that building."[2]

Sophomore Jalen Brunson was a problem in that game, scoring 24 points for the Wildcats, but Chrabascz had 8 assists to support his 7 rebounds for the Dawgs.

With the nation's consciousness squarely on the Bulldogs, they went to Cincinnati four days later and impressively knocked off

Xavier 88–79 to clinch second place in the Big East. Butler shot 58 percent in the second half and 54 percent on the game to run its record to 23–6.

The regular season finale was at home against Seton Hall, which had fallen in January to the Dawgs 61–54. The Pirates' Ángel Delgado had pulled down 22 rebounds in that game, and in the finale his 20 points and 16 rebounds brought Seton Hall from a 10-point deficit with seven minutes to play and gave the Pirates a 70–64 victory.

36 | HAS BUTLER'S RISE AFFECTED IU?

WHILE BUTLER WAS PRODUCING A decade of major accomplishments, its neighbor to the south was going through troubling times, struggles that saw IU fire two coaches and battle back from NCAA sanctions.

Indiana and Butler have never had what most consider a bitter rivalry such as IU shares with Purdue. IU and Butler didn't schedule each other between 1971 and 1991. They presently meet every two years in the Crossroads Classic, and IU has won four of the last seven games against Butler. Boasting five NCAA championships, Indiana's tradition is superior to most universities, but if success is based on what has been done lately, the Bulldogs hold a bit of an edge.

Whether Butler has played any role in Indiana's recent problems is debatable, but certain things have become points of interest:

Many Indiana fans have openly wished Stevens might get tired of the Boston Celtics and want to return to his home state as IU coach.

Likewise, IU backers who longed for Coach Tom Crean's firing often spoke about what a good job Holtmann was doing at Butler.

While Stevens constantly supports the Butler program and praises his former employer, former IU coach Bob Knight remarked of his former superiors, "I hope they're all dead."[1]

Although Indiana has won two Big Ten championships in the past five seasons, the Hoosiers have never won the Big Ten Tournament in its twenty years. During Butler's trips to the NCAA Tournament's title games in 2010 and 2011, the Hoosiers didn't even make the tournament field.

While Indiana has enjoyed a long relationship with the Big Ten, Butler advanced from the mid-majors to the Big East Conference five years ago and has a pair of second-place finishes there. Twenty-five years ago, a Butler home game might draw five thousand fans. Parking was free, and you could pick any seat in the house. Now tickets cost several times as much and almost every game is a sellout.

Prior to the hiring of Archie Miller as IU coach in the summer of 2017, seats high in Simon Skjodt Assembly Hall were often plentiful.

Whether the escalation of Butler's program has contributed to IU's situation is questionable. But one should note that the Hoosiers didn't recruit in-state players Hayward or Howard, didn't seem to think Dunham or six-ten Smith were worth having, and didn't have much interest in Graves, the fifth-leading scorer in Butler history, who lived less than an hour away from Bloomington.

37 | NO ORDINARY ROAD TRIP

LONG AIRPLANE FLIGHTS HOME ARE never fun following a loss, but Butler's return from a 76–73 upset at the hands of St. John's on December 29, 2016, resulted in their biggest scare of the season.

The Bulldogs traveling party was about twenty-five minutes into a flight out of New York when their plane lost cabin pressure and oxygen masks dropped out of the ceiling. Cabin lights went out, and the aircraft dropped about 25,000 feet in a ten-minute period, leveling off at 10,000 feet. Uncertain of their fate, some of those aboard texted family members about the dilemma.

"For many of us who are experienced flyers, and certainly for those inexperienced flyers, it was a terrifying experience, primarily because it was the unknown," Holtmann said. "We hadn't been through it before. We hadn't been through an experience like that. We hadn't lost cabin pressure before. We just didn't know what to expect. I think that shook up a lot of guys, particularly those who were on only their fifth or sixth time flying. If it was my thousandth time flying, I'd be shook up as well."

Holtmann said the passengers could hear the pilots' voices as well as the engines. "I think the only guy who was in a peaceful state was our athletic director [Barry Collier]," he said.

The plane landed in Pittsburgh, and the team spent the night there before boarding another plane home.

A month later the University of Michigan team plane slid off the runway at a Detroit-area airport and delayed the club's arrival for the Big Ten Tournament in Washington, DC. No serious injuries were involved, and Michigan went on to win the tournament.

38 | HELP FROM THE OUTSIDE

BASKETBALL RECRUITING HAS TAKEN ON a new dimension in recent years, and Butler coaches have utilized different methods of bringing in talent than those used by Hinkle. For example, Butler has received major contributions from players who started at other colleges.

Butler's coaches, from Lickliter to Holtmann, kept the program strong by attracting transfers. One of the best was Mike Green, who transferred from Towson in 2006 and started seventy games for the Bulldogs while leading them to the preseason NIT and Great Alaska Shootout championships. Green was the Horizon League's Newcomer of the Year in 2007 and the Horizon's Player of the Year in 2008. He was the first Butler player to record 400 points, 200 rebounds, and100 assists in a season.

Arriving at Butler the same year as Green was Pete Campbell, a transfer from Indiana University–Purdue University Fort Wayne (IPFW). Campbell made 48 percent of his three-point attempts during his Butler career and scored 26 points in twenty minutes in an NCAA Tournament win over South Alabama.

A third transfer on those Butler teams was Julian Betko, who started his career at Clemson in 2005 and played in 103 consecutive games as a Bulldog. All three players arrived under Lickliter and also played for Stevens.

Avery Jukes played part of one season at Alabama before transferring to Butler in 2007. He played a pivotal role on the 2010 Final Four team as a backup to foul-prone Matt Howard.

Ronald Nored didn't play at another college but had given a verbal commitment to Western Kentucky. When the Hilltoppers changed coaches, Nored changed his mind and came to Butler.

The Bulldogs had Arkansas transfer Rotnei Clarke for only one season as was the case with St. Bonaventure transfer Jordan Gathers. Tyler Lewis, a stalwart on the 2017 team, left North Carolina State for two seasons at Butler, the same period of time Indiana transfer Austin Etherington spent as a Dawg.

Holtmann and his staff paved the way for Butler to have an outstanding season in 2017, one that included two wins over Villanova. Despite losing Jones and Dunham, the Bulldogs improved their depth and overall skill by adding transfers Avery Woodson and Kethan Savage.

Woodson had already graduated from Memphis and had a season of eligibility remaining, allowing him to play immediately at his new school. Woodson made forty-five starts at Memphis, making 41 percent of his 341 three-point shots. He was equally prolific at Butler, becoming a late-season starter and making more than 40 percent of his threes.

Slowed by an early season injury, Savage became a late-season starter, allowing Holtmann to use Martin and Lewis off the bench. Kethan had played three seasons at George Washington (GW) and sat out a season after enrolling at Butler.

Savage's GW teammate Paul Jorgensen, a six-foot-two guard, also sat out a year and became eligible with the Bulldogs for the 2017–18 season. Jorgensen had averaged sixteen minutes a game while helping GW to the 2016 NIT title.

39 | KELAN MARTIN STRONG IN ANY ROLE

THE GENERAL CONSENSUS IN BASKETBALL is that a team's leading scorer should be in the starting lineup. Otherwise, conjectures abound as to why not. Perhaps he has broken team rules, missed classes, or shown a lack of effort in practice.

When Butler took the court at Marquette on February 7, 2017, the Bulldogs lineup consisted of Chrabascz, Wideman, Savage, Baldwin, and Woodson. Kelan Martin, who had scored 22 points in Butler's first meeting against Marquette, was on the bench.

Butler won the game 68–65, and Fox Sports analyst Steve Lappas was almost beside himself hinting that there had to be a subversive reason Martin wasn't starting. Holtmann insisted all was routine, other than his desire that Martin become more of a complete player.

Martin had come off the bench during the first half of the 2015–16 season while leading the Dawgs in scoring fourteen times. He hit Georgetown with 35 points and was All-Big East second team while scoring 16 points a game. In 2016–17 he scored 30 against Central Arkansas and 28 against Indiana. At six feet seven and 220 pounds, the junior from Louisville Ballard High was a scoring threat no matter how Holtmann deployed him. In a two-game swing that led to road victories over Villanova and Xavier, he scored 22 and 25 points, respectfully, and led Butler's rebounding in both games. By his senior season, Martin had become one of the top scorers in the Big East, averaging more than 20 points. He scored 37 against Marquette and 34 against Xavier.

Former Indiana coach Crean, who knew Kelan's parents when he was on the staff at Western Kentucky and they were in college there, praised Martin as a "big-time player."

"He can really score, a great line driver, a very efficient shooter," Crean said. "He goes both ways, takes big shots, wants to take big shots. He's very athletic; he's really improved."[1]

Martin is a versatile scorer, one who can pop jumpers from well beyond the three-point line or can drive into the lane and launch accurate shots in traffic. He grabbed 11 rebounds against Seton Hall, playing against one of the nation's top rebounders, Ángel Delgado. He also had 10 boards against Georgetown.

Working off the bench with senior point guard Tyler Lewis, the pairing was jokingly referred to as Martin and Lewis, alluding to the 1950s comedy team of Dean Martin and Jerry Lewis.

Martin said neither Kentucky nor Louisville recruited him, although he is only one of three Ballard players to score 2,000 career points. He was a first-team All-State performer and a member of the Kentucky All-Star team that played Indiana in the summer.

Kelan's father, Kenneth, played for Ballard when it won a Kentucky state championship and went on to Kentucky Wesleyan, where his team won an NCAA Division II championship. Later, Kenneth coached middle school boys in Louisville, including future NBA star Rajon Rondo. Kelan's mother, Kristie, was a star at Ballard and helped Western Kentucky to a runner-up finish in the NCAA Women's Tournament. Ballard has a rich basketball tradition, and Martin was preceded there by Tennessee All-American Alan Houston and Jeff Lamp, a teammate of Ralph Sampson at Virginia.

Butler recruited Kelan early and he liked the match.

40 | X MARKS THE SPOT OF BUTLER'S BIGGEST RIVAL

BUTLER'S PRIMARY RIVAL HAS CHANGED from decade to decade depending on the caliber of competition Butler was playing at the time.

During the first half of the twentieth century, Wabash carried on a thing with Butler, which was barely an hour away from the Crawfordsville school. The Bulldogs and Little Giants played basketball twice a year, and Butler currently owns an 86–33 lead in the series, which included an exhibition game in 2016. While Wabash competed as an independent, Butler also had a home-and-home series with six other schools in the Indiana Collegiate Conference (ICC): DePauw, Indiana State, Ball State, Evansville, Valparaiso, and St. Joseph's.

Butler has a lopsided record in basketball against five of those six schools, the exception being Evansville. The Purple Aces hold a 62–57 edge in that series, and their last meeting was a 69–59 Butler victory in December 2013. Butler's Final Four team of 2010–11 lost to the Aces 71–68.

Butler's most memorable game against Wabash was a 110–108 loss in five overtimes during the 1959–60 season. During the early 1960s, a giant *W* was burned into the middle of Butler's football field, a prank blamed on Wabash students.

The Butler-Evansville rivalry peaked in the late '50s and early '60s when Evansville was an NCAA Division II power and Butler played a Division I schedule. During the 1958 season, the Bulldogs' Plump scored 41 points in a 101–76 victory over the Aces in the fieldhouse. Plump made all seventeen of his free throws that night, still a Butler record.

Butler's 1962 NCAA team beat Evansville twice during a thirteen-game winning streak. Three years later, when the Aces had future NBA star Jerry Sloan, they whipped the Dawgs twice.

Most of those in-state rivalries faded away when the Bulldogs joined the new Midwestern City Conference in 1979. The MCC later became the Midwestern Collegiate Conference and then the Horizon League, and by the time the Bulldogs left that circuit in 2012, they had formed several new rivalries, especially with Wright State of Dayton, Ohio.

Butler and Xavier University (XU) first played in 1936 when Xavier posted a 28–26 victory in Cincinnati. Butler won the second meeting four years later, but the teams didn't play each other again for thirty-six years. At the end of the 2017 season, Xavier owned a 38–20 lead.

The schools started regular play when both became inaugural members of the MCC. Xavier left that league in 1995 and joined the A-10; Butler spent one season in the A-10 before three new schools were added to the Big East: Xavier, Butler, and Creighton. Butler and Xavier split two games during their short time in the A-10.

The three Big East newcomers proved to be formidable opposition in their new league. After losing fourteen Big East games in its inaugural season, Butler tied for second in its second season and tied for fourth in 2016. Xavier tied for third, then was sixth and second in its first three seasons, respectively.

The Butler-Xavier rivalry was stepped up during a nonconference game at Hinkle during the 2009–10 season. Hayward made a spectacular play at the end of the game for a 69–68 Butler victory. A clock controversy intervened, and, while the official ruling appeared to be correct, several Xavier players left the court feeling cheated.

At the turn of the century, Xavier's successes probably exceeded Butler's, and Bulldog coach Matta left his alma mater to coach Xavier. Matta, who went 24–8 in his one season at Butler, coached three seasons at Xavier before being hired at Ohio State.

Butler and Xavier were natural rivals in the Big East because it was the third conference to claim them both, and because both were in large cities only hours apart. The fact that they also competed for the same recruits only fired up their feelings. Both especially wanted the services of Indianapolis Park Tudor graduate Trevon Bluiett, an All-Big East player at XU. Bloomington South product Dee Davis was a thorn in Butler's side for four years. Cincinnati natives Joel Cornette and Nate Fowler got away from Xavier and became Bulldogs.

The Musketeers defeated the Bulldogs in six of their first nine meetings as Big East foes. The Bulldogs were seeded second in the 2017 Big East Tournament in Madison Square Garden. They had defeated the Musketeers twice during the season but lost their third meeting in the Garden, 62–57. The victory was probably necessary if Xavier was to make the NCAA Tournament. The Musketeers, who lost five straight games late in the season, finished with a 24–14 record.

Asked if Xavier had become Butler's principal rival, Holtmann responded, "I think it probably is in terms of our fans. There is a combativeness among our fan bases that is unlike most other programs."

41 | DAWGS REACH THE SWEET SIXTEEN

BUTLER ENTERED THE 2017 NCAA Tournament as the No. 4 seed in the South Regional, which marked the highest seed in the school's history. The selection committee paired the Dawgs against Winthrop, a small but traditionally strong school from Rock Hill, South Carolina.

The Big East placed seven schools in the tournament, headed by overall No. 1 seed Villanova, the defending national champion. Butler had the next highest seed among conference schools. Others representing the Big East were Creighton (6), Seton Hall (9), Marquette (10), and Xavier (11). Providence was one of four schools that needed an extra game to make the final sixty-four teams, but the Friars lost to the University of Southern California (USC) Trojans.

Butler's list of victims included ten teams that made the sixty-eight-team tournament field: Villanova, No. 2 seed Arizona, Creighton, No. 6 Cincinnati, Marquette, No. 8 Northwestern, No. 9 Vanderbilt, Seton Hall, No. 13 Bucknell, and Providence.

Playing an afternoon game against Winthrop in Milwaukee, Wisconsin, the Bulldogs had few problems disposing of their first-round foe, 76–64. In the second round, they were pitted against a thirty-game winner, Middle Tennessee State, a tenth seed that had upset No. 5 Minnesota in its opener. The Blue

Raiders were confident and experienced, having knocked off Michigan State in 2016.

But the Bulldogs outlasted their Tennessee foe 74–65 and advanced to the Sweet Sixteen in Memphis, Tennessee, against top-seeded North Carolina. Butler and Xavier were the only Big East schools to reach the round of sixteen following Villanova's upset loss to Wisconsin and defeats by Creighton, Seton Hall, Marquette, and Providence. Wisconsin's style of play, featuring a rugged defense and patient offense, reminded many of Butler.

The South Regional featured teams claiming twenty-four NCAA championships: UCLA with eleven, Kentucky with eight, and North Carolina with five. Although underdogs against top-seeded North Carolina, the Bulldogs had a number of supporters who thought they would win, including CBS analysts Clark Kellogg and Charles Barkley. Two years earlier, Holtmann's first team had knocked off the Tar Heels in Nassau, 74–66. Stevens's last Butler team had also beaten North Carolina in Hawaii, 82–71, in a game that wasn't that close.

Unfortunately for Butler, North Carolina came out smoking and took a 20-point lead during the first half while shooting 52 percent. The Bulldogs made a couple of runs at the Heels and even outscored them by 4 points in the second half, but North Carolina turned in one of its better efforts and won 93–80. Its superiority was most evident on the backboards, where it had a 38–26 advantage. Chrabascz closed his career with a superb effort for the Dawgs, contributing 21 points, 7 rebounds, and 4 assists.

The Butler program went into the off-season with great expectations for the near future. Although not unexpected, by mid-June fans received bad news. Holtmann had been hired as head coach at Ohio State to replace former Butler player and coach Matta. Collier, again staying within the Butler family, brought in former Bulldog LaVall Jordan as head coach.

Gordon Hayward drives against Mason Plumlee in Butler's 61–59 loss to Duke in the 2010 national championship game in Indianapolis. Hayward's midcourt shot at the buzzer was inches away from giving the Bulldogs a national championship.

Facing, Brad Stevens, kneeling in front of the Butler bench, left a promising career with Eli Lilly to become a volunteer coach with the Bulldogs in 2000. In 2008 he was named Butler's head coach and led his first team to a 30–4 record. Two years later the Bulldogs played for the national championship and the following season they again reached the title game.

Todd Lickliter had a successful six-year reign as the Bulldogs coach with his teams posting a 131–61 record. When he left to become coach at Iowa in 2007, new coach Brad Stevens inherited one of the nation's top backcourts in A. J. Graves and Mike Green.

Facing, Guard A. J. Graves drives against Old Dominion in an NCAA regional game in 2007. The Bulldogs triumphed 57–46 and then sidelined Maryland 62–59. Butler was ousted in the Sweet Sixteen by third-seeded Florida, 65–57. Graves went on to become the fifth-leading scorer in Butler history.

BUTLER
4

A. J. Graves followed his brother, Matt, to Butler University and scored 1,807 points between 2005 and 2008. Other schools, including Indiana, apparently thought A. J. was too small to play major college basketball. A superb shooter, the younger Graves made 91 of his first 92 free throws at the start of the 2006–07 season, including a string of 63 in a row.

Andrew Smith scored 1,147 points and made 53 percent of his shots during a four-year career that ended in 2013. Tragically, Andrew died at age 25 after a two-year battle with cancer. Smith's wife, Samantha, launched an internet campaign called "Kicking Cancer with the Smiths" that outlined the couple's courageous fight against impossible odds.

Brad Stevens may have been mistaken for a teenager when he became coach of the Bulldogs, but he wasn't docile on the bench. Director of athletics Barry Collier said Stevens is a great communicator: "He can speak to 3-year-olds and 103-year-olds."

Facing, Roosevelt Jones, shown driving against DePaul, was one of the most unique players in college basketball. He could score by almost every method, yet never took the conventional jump shot. As Purdue coach Matt Painter said, "He can't shoot! Period! He can't shoot, and he's a great player."

BUTLER
21

Brad Stevens, being interviewed here by ESPN's Jay Bilas, turned down numerous college coaching jobs before agreeing to become head coach of the Boston Celtics. Butler sports information director Jim McGrath called it one of the worst days of his life.

Facing, Kellen Dunham played four seasons for the Bulldogs under three different coaches: Brad Stevens, Brandon Miller, and Chris Holtmann. Butler won eighty-six games during that period as the sharpshooting Dunham scored 1,946 points. The only Bulldogs to score more were Chad Tucker and Darrin Fitzgerald.

23

Chris Holtmann left a head coaching position at Gardner-Webb to take an assistant's job at Butler. After being named to lead the Bulldogs, he took them to three NCAA Tournaments in three years, including the Sweet Sixteen in 2017. Holtmann then was hired as head coach at Ohio State.

Facing, Roosevelt Jones finds some room in the foul lane to launch a one-handed push shot against Georgetown. Jones missed the entire 2012–13 season with an injury, and the Bulldogs posted a 14–17 record without him. When he returned, Butler went 45–22 the following two seasons.

21
GEORGETOWN
5

BUTLER
34

Chris Holtmann offers advice from the bench during a Big East game in Hinkle Fieldhouse. Holtmann won multiple coaching honors after his team posted a 25–9 record in 2017 and beat defending national champion Villanova twice.

Facing, Pete Campbell became one of the best outside shooters in the school's history after transferring from IPFW. "When people ask who was the best shooter you've seen at Butler, Pete's the name that pops into my mind," said former sports information director Jim McGrath. Against Old Dominion he erupted for 9 points in a ninety-one-second span.

Butler's director of athletics, Barry Collier (*left*), is joined by sports information director Jim McGrath during a press conference. Collier appointed Brad Stevens, Brandon Miller, Chris Holtmann, and LaVall Jordan in succession to be Bulldogs' head coaches.

Facing, Barry Collier's last game as Butler coach was an overtime loss to Florida in the 2000 NCAA Tournament. The Gators' Mike Miller hit a shot at the buzzer that still grates on Collier and many Butler fans.

Roosevelt Jones drives for a score in a Big East game against Xavier at Hinkle Fieldhouse. Although standing only six feet four, Jones was a prolific rebounder who had a nose for the basketball. He made only one three-point shot at Butler, that coming on a midcourt heave that beat the halftime buzzer.

Facing, Director of athletics Barry Collier speaks at a Butler press conference. Collier is largely responsible for reviving Butler's basketball program in the early 2000s. The former coach returned to his alma mater after six years as coach at Nebraska.

Former Bulldogs Joel Cornette, LaVall Jordan, and Matt Graves (*left to right*) huddle on the sideline at Hinkle Fieldhouse. All were former assistant coaches, and Jordan was named head coach when Chris Holtmann went to Ohio State in 2017.

LaVall Jordan (*right*), shown with Barry Collier at his introductory press conference, was head coach at Milwaukee-Wisconsin before being named to coach the Bulldogs. He previously served as an assistant at Michigan.

LaVall Jordan voices his appreciation at being named coach of his alma mater after Chris Holtmann accepted the head coaching job at Ohio State following the 2017 season. Holtmann had succeeded another former Butler head coach, Thad Matta.

Facing, Trip, the latest of three four-legged Butler mascots, is dressed in his game attire. Trip also serves the university as a recruiting tool and occasionally delivers letters of acceptance to incoming Butler students.

Traditionally, players pet Trip, Butler's bulldog mascot, during the pregame introductions. Then, knowing a large bone lies in his future, Trip races the length of the floor to claim his reward.

Facing, Michael Kaltenmark is Trip's best two-legged friend and sometimes takes the Bulldogs' mascot to work. Trip's predecessor, Blue II, was a big hit at the Final Four in 2010 and 2011. Kaltenmark claims Trip is "Final Four–ready whenever the team is."

LOCKHART

Andrew Chrabascz started for four seasons as a six-foot-seven forward. One of the nation's best passing big men, Chrabascz eased Butler's move from the Horizon League to the Big East. He closed his career with a 21-point, 7-rebound, 4-assist game against North Carolina.

Shelvin Mack, a major force in Butler's successive trips to the national title game, was a prolific driver and outside shooter. Butler recruiters plucked him out of Lexington, Kentucky, beating the home state school, University of Kentucky, to a future NBA pro.

12
55

Joel Cornette (33) died in 2016 of coronary artery disease at age 35. Cornette made a dunk shot in the final seconds to beat Indiana 66–64 in December 2001. The Hoosiers went on to play in the national title game while the Bulldogs enjoyed a 26–6 season.

Facing, Gordon Hayward launches a shot over Kyle Singler (12) and Brian Zoubek (55) of Duke in the 2010 NCAA title game. Hayward turned professional after that season and became an all-pro player with the Utah Jazz. On becoming a free agent in 2017, he joined former coach Brad Stevens with the Boston Celtics.

Kamar Baldwin drives for the basket after stealing the ball from Villanova's Josh Hart late in Butler's win over the nation's No. 1 team at Hinkle Fieldhouse. The Bulldogs also defeated Villanova later in the 2017 season in Philadelphia.

Head coach LaVall Jordan conducts a recent practice session in Hinkle Fieldhouse. Jordan retained three starters from Chris Holtmann's final team while losing six seniors.

Rotnei Clarke of the Bulldogs drives past Indiana's Victor Oladipo during the Bulldogs' 88–86 upset of the No. 1 Hoosiers in December 2012. Clarke, who was a high school legend in Oklahoma, played one season at Butler.

Facing, Ronald Nored's defense was a major factor in Butler making the Final Four twice. He enrolled at Butler after previously committing to play at Western Kentucky. When the Hilltoppers changed coaches, he opted to come to Butler instead. Here he drives past Duke's Lance Thomas (42) as Butler's Avery Jukes watches.

BUTLER
24

BUTLER
4

Shelvin Mack, one of two Bulldogs from the 2010 team to advance to the NBA, fights for position. Mack and Gordon Hayward were later teammates with the Utah Jazz.

Facing, Brandon Miller (4), who later became Butler's head coach, led the Bulldogs in scoring in 2003. A native of New Castle, Indiana, he served as an assistant coach at Butler, Ohio State, and Illinois.

Joel Cornette jostles for position while playing for the Bulldogs. He was an assistant coach at Butler before his tragic death at age 35.

Todd Lickliter makes a point to the official during a 53–52 victory over Miami of Ohio in the 2006 NIT. Lickliter's Dawgs lost a four-point game to Florida State in the next game and finished the season with a 20–13 record.

42 | LAVALL JORDAN TAKES OVER BULLDOGS

WHEN AN ATHLETIC PROGRAM GOES through seven head coaches in a nineteen-year period, it customarily means the program is struggling. When Butler named Jordan as its seventh mentor since 2000, that was not the case. In fact, the Bulldogs had won 421 games over that span when the former Butler player became head coach in the summer of 2017.

Jordan possessed the common denominator for consideration as head Dawg: he was a former Bulldog (1998–2001) and assistant coach (under Lickliter). Collier, the first of those seven coaches and present athletic director, has stuck to in-house candidates since starting with Stevens in 2007.

Following Collier were Matta, Lickliter, Stevens, Miller, and Holtmann. When major colleges needed a coach, they almost inevitably looked Butler's way. Matta, whose lone Butler team won twenty-four games, went to Ohio State by way of Xavier. Lickliter went to Iowa after directing Butler to twenty-nine victories in 2007.

Stevens, of course, won thirty games as a rookie coach and thirty-three games in his third season. Miller won only fourteen games before stepping down for undisclosed health reasons, and

Holtmann's work was such that Ohio State quickly hired him to replace Matta in 2017.

Jordon was the most valuable player on Matta's 2001 team and served three years as a Butler assistant. He then spent six seasons as an assistant to John Beilein at Michigan as the Wolverines reached the national title game in 2013. While LaVall was in Ann Arbor, the Wolverines averaged twenty-four wins a season. Jordan's first head coaching experience was at Milwaukee in 2016, and he took a team seeded tenth to the championship game of the Horizon League Tournament.

As had been the case in prior years with coaching changes, Jordan's first Butler team was given little respect entering his inaugural season. The Dawgs were picked to finish eighth among ten Big East teams in a preseason poll. They had finished second in Holtmann's final season with a senior-laden team. Their major departure was forward Chrabascz, but Lewis, Woodson, and Savage also were gone.

Jordan retained starters Wideman, Martin, and Baldwin, while Fowler, McDermott, and Henry Baddley also returned. George Washington transfer Paul Jorgensen became eligible.

Not only did Butler lose Holtmann, but a vapor trail of talent followed him. Holtmann assistants Johnson, Pedon, and Schrage took their reputations as strong recruiters to Columbus. Kyle Young, considered the top player in Holtmann's last recruiting class, opted out of his commitment to Butler and enrolled at Ohio State. Then Cooper Neese changed his mind and decided to spurn the Bulldogs in favor of Indiana State.

Suddenly, what had been considered the top recruiting class in Butler history lacked a single commitment when the 2017–18 season opened. The Bulldogs lost early in the season to Maryland and Texas but stunned Holtmann's Ohio State team in the PK80-Phil Knight Invitational in Portland, Oregon. Butler trailed the Big Ten team by 15 points with five minutes to play before erupting for a one-point victory in overtime.

Butler entered the 2018 Big East season with a 10–3 record and a forty-three-game winning streak at home against non-conference opponents. Purdue planted an 82–67 loss on the Bulldogs in the Crossroads Classic, but five days later they beat Western Illinois by 61 points.

"It might be the most coachable group I've been around," Jordan said on Media Day, October 19, 2017.

43 | TALENT IS EVERYWHERE, JUST FIND IT

BUTLER'S MOVE TO THE BIG East Conference in 2013 meant that the basketball coaches faced some major changes in their responsibilities. No longer could they be satisfied with bringing in players good enough for the Horizon League. Now they would have to locate players with enough talent to play a couple of levels higher than the school's onetime mid-major rivals.

Not only would they have to scout the better talent, but the coaches would have to spread their wings and find it in sections of the country where Butler has been less likely to land players. More importantly, they would have to sell these players on playing at Butler.

Back in the old Hinkle days, Butler landed the bulk of its players from Indianapolis or across Indiana. A few came great distances to play at Butler, such as Johnny Jones of Washington, DC, or Rolf van Rijn of The Netherlands, but the bulk were Hoosier born and bred: Gerry Williams of Shortridge, Ken Pennington of Warren Central, Orville Bose of Hymera, Larry Shade of Seymour, and Jeff Blue of Bainbridge. Many of them were undersized guards or sawed-off centers ignored by the big schools. Often it didn't matter, as when the six-foot-four Pennington scored 36 against Indiana's six-foot-ten Walt Bellamy.

The move to the Big East meant that the coaches would have to concentrate more on the East Coast, where better players might consider the Bulldogs because they would be meeting Eastern schools. Naturally, more money would be spent recruiting, and with Butler being in a better league, more prospects would be attracted to a campus visit.

Butler had a head start because two players recruited for a Horizon League team, Jones and Dunham, became Big East All-Stars. Chrabascz, the best player in Rhode Island, responded to Stevens's sales pitch and became a Bulldog star.

Chrabascz was plucked away from Providence coach Ed Cooley, who had to contend with him for the next four years in the Big East. Said Cooley, "I'm a big fan of his, I really am. He chose a great school, chose a great system. A lot of offense is run through him. They give him a lot of freedom to play, and I think that freedom to play helped him grow.[1]

"He's really a tough matchup inside," Cooley added. "Outside he's probably an underrated passer. He's one of the best passing big men in the country."

Butler is a more attractive choice than it was before its dual Final Fours. As former assistant coach Johnson said, "Now that we're in the Big East, a lot of guys are willing to listen more. Knowing that we went to the Final Four they'll listen, and with the Big East they want to come and see us. I think that helps out a lot."

Mike Schrage, another assistant under Holtmann, believes one of Butler's biggest selling points also is its oldest. "I think the biggest litmus test is when we have a kid come on campus; we bring them into Hinkle. You can tell by their reaction that they appreciate it," Schrage said. "It doesn't have to be all bells and whistles that a new arena is going to have. It was updated a few years ago, but you're going to appreciate it for the history. It's a living museum."[2]

Stevens once said, "Not every recruit who walks into Hinkle is going to say, Wow! But the ones who do are the ones we want."[3]

Schrage would agree, noting that when a recruit walks into Hinkle, his impression is reflected in his eyes. "It's a special place," he said.

Butler's recruiting base is widespread but centers on Indiana and surrounding states. Indiana was represented in the 2017 roster by Schererville's Tyler Wideman, Pendleton's Sean McDermott, walk-on Steven Bennett, and redshirt Joey Brunk. There were two players from Ohio, and one each from Mississippi, Georgia, North Carolina, Missouri, Virginia, Kentucky, Rhode Island, and New York City.

44 | HINKLE FIELDHOUSE: A HISTORIC SITE

BUTLER UNIVERSITY, FOUNDED IN 1855, was originally named North Western Christian University and located at Thirteenth Street and College Avenue. Ovid Butler, the school's founder, donated the property.

Butler was established by members of the Christian Church (Disciples of Christ), but that church never held controlling interest in the school. Butler was the first college in Indiana, and the third in the nation, to admit both men and women.

In 1885 the school was renamed after its founder, and the campus was moved to a twenty-five-acre spot in Irvington, a suburb of Indianapolis on the east side. The Bona Thompson Library at Downey and University Avenues is the only building remaining from the original Irvington campus. The administration realized the need for a larger campus following World War I, and the school was relocated to its present site at Fairview Park, a onetime amusement park on the city's northwest side.

Classes began there in 1928, when the first building, a large classroom facility named Jordan Hall, was constructed. That same year Butler Fieldhouse was completed along Forty-Ninth Street at the north edge of the new campus. Also in the works was Butler Bowl, built into the ground alongside the fieldhouse and originally designed to have thirty-six thousand seats. The field is still used, but all seating east of the playing field was removed and replaced by housing in 2006. The seating at the Bowl had been downsized to twenty thousand in the mid-1950s.

Butler Fieldhouse came to be known not only as the home of the Bulldogs but as the site for the Indiana High School Basketball Tournament. The aura of the fieldhouse played a major role in Indiana becoming the center of basketball enthusiasm across the nation.

Renamed for Hinkle in 1966, the fieldhouse was the largest basketball arena in the county until 1950. Originally featuring fifteen thousand bench seats, it was reduced to ten thousand in the early 1990s when more comfortable seating was installed. Now the sixth oldest arena currently in use, it has undergone a couple of major facelifts.

The basketball court was once laid out from east to west along the length of the building, but in 1933 it was adjusted to run north and south, placing most of the seats on the sides of the court. The high school tournament was held there from 1928 until 1971, except when it was used as military barracks during World War II.

The massive, but somewhat dank, arena was overhauled in 1989 at a cost of $1.5 million. It was renovated again beginning in 2011 and capacity was further reduced to 9,100. An auxiliary gymnasium remains at the west end of the building, but a swimming pool that once adjoined it has been removed and replaced by an indoor structure housing athletic offices, an academic center, and training facilities. The latest renovation in 2014 cost $36 million.

Hinkle Fieldhouse has been home to numerous nonathletic events, including track meets in which the legendary Jesse Owens competed. It has seen presidential visits by Herbert Hoover, Dwight D. Eisenhower, Richard Nixon, Gerald Ford, George H. W. Bush, and Bill Clinton. Billy Graham has preached there, and an NBA team, the Indianapolis Olympians, played there. It has also hosted a circus, a bicycle race, a roller derby, and a tennis match between Bill Tilden and Jack Kramer. Most of all, hundreds of great basketball players have played there, from George Mikan to Oscar Robertson to Gordon Hayward.

The fieldhouse may be most famous for being one of the sites of the 1986 movie *Hoosiers*, often called the best sports movie of all time. The film was based on tiny Milan High School's state championship, won on the same court on Plump's last-second shot. The production crew spent a week preparing for the final scenes, and producers hoped the public might fill the building for background crowd shots. Instead, only a few thousand fans came, and they were subsequently shuffled into different seating areas to simulate a full house.[1]

45 | BUTLER BOWL IS FULL OF HISTORY

BUTLER BOWL, ONCE INTENDED TO be one of the larger football stadiums in the Midwest, was downsized in 2006 into a picturesque facility that houses the university's football and soccer teams. Located on the northeast edge of Hinkle Fieldhouse, the field was home to the Bulldogs in the years when they competed against Red Grange and Illinois and the Four Horsemen of Notre Dame.

Butler Bowl was constructed in 1928, the same year as the fieldhouse, and was built into a hillside running alongside Boulevard Place. The original bowl had seating for thirty-six thousand fans and could have been expanded to a capacity of seventy-two thousand. At the time, Butler was weighing the possibility of becoming a major football school.

The Bulldogs beat Franklin 55–0 in the inaugural game there in 1928.

Until 1955 another sixteen thousand seats were located at the south end of the field but were replaced with the construction of the Hilton U. Brown Theatron, an outdoor entertainment center with a stage circled by theater seats. Off-Broadway productions known as Starlight Musicals were held there for years.

The football seating was showing its age when it was dismantled in 2006, being reduced to 5,647 seats. At that time almost all the seats were on the east side, where fans had to look into the sun. A limited seating area on the west side was beautified and expanded, and a modern 3,330 square-foot press box replaced a cramped one that had been used for years. A small section for visiting fans was built on the east side of the field. Removing the old bleachers made it possible to construct the Butler Apartment Village along Boulevard Place.

Beginning in 1958 Butler won five straight ICC football championships under Hinkle, losing only one game over a three-year period.

46 | STEVENS LEADS BY EXAMPLE

WHEN STEVENS TOOK OVER AS coach of the Boston Celtics in 2013, the seventeen-time NBA champions were coming off a 41–40 season record that was well below the expectations of Boston fans. Stevens's move was a surprise to both college and NBA fans, who assumed the young Butler coach would go on to win maybe eight hundred games either with the Bulldogs or some other college.

A number of successful collegiate coaches had tried the NBA, and most of them had returned to the college ranks after unsuccessful ventures. Rick Pitino, Lon Kruger, John Calipari, Tim Floyd, P. J. Carlisimo, Reggie Theus, Leonard Hamilton, and Jerry Tarkianian were prime examples with only Carlisimo winning a single playoff game in the NBA. Yet, Stevens was so impressive at Butler that many felt he would do well.

Matt Norlander, writing for CBS Sports on Stevens's arrival in Boston, saw Stevens as a good hire by the Celtics. "He's a different kind of coach who's won under unprecedented circumstances," Norlander wrote. "[He] has a tactical approach to the game that's new age and in line with evolving NBA concepts of how to build a team and where to emphasize what components in order to win." And if he succeeds in the NBA where other college coaches have failed? Norlander adds, "He'll just be Brad

Stevens, proving people wrong again and basically looking like one of the most competent basketball minds of his generation."[1]

The Celtics learned quickly what the Bulldogs already knew: that Stevens had a brilliant mind, worked tirelessly, and was an outstanding communicator. His first pro team had a mere 25–57 record, but as he gradually cleaned house and implemented his basketball theories, the Celtics' rebuilding took hold. They went 40–42 in his third season and were at or near the top of the Eastern Division throughout all of the 2017 campaign.

Working with general manager Danny Ainge, Stevens helped acquire five-foot-nine All-Star Isaiah Thomas from Phoenix after the stylish guard was drafted sixtieth in the 2011 draft.

The Celtics acquired Al Horford in a 2016 trade with Atlanta, Jae Crowder in a 2017 deal with Dallas, and Tyler Zeller in a 2014 trade with Cleveland. They got Kelly Olynyk in a trade shortly after he joined the league in 2013. Marcus Smart was drafted out of Oklahoma State in 2014.

Boston's biggest star when Stevens arrived was controversial guard Rajon Rondo. He was shipped to Dallas in 2014 with Crowder proving a worthy replacement.

Although the NBA All-Star game is largely an exhibition, Stevens was chosen to coach the East in only his fourth year in the league. It is widely speculated that he will coach the US Olympic team someday.

"It's become increasingly clear Stevens is up to the task," wrote Ben Dowsett of *Basketball Insiders*.[2]

The former Butler coach has hit it off with his players, which isn't always a given in the NBA. College basketball often revolves around coaches while the NBA spotlight is on players. If there are disputes in college, the player sometimes transfers. If an NBA star has a problem with his coach, it is usually the coach who goes.

Former Celtics guard Avery Bradley was asked to identify Stevens's greatest strength: "Leading by example," he told Dowsett. "A lot of the things he does, I think (they) rub off on us. Him preparing for each game, we see how hard he works and it makes us want to go out there and not only be prepared for him, but be prepared for the team," Bradley continued.[3]

One of Stevens's strengths is designing out-of-bounds plays. He had several that worked for the Bulldogs, including a full-court series of passes that preceded Hahn's game-winning three-pointer against Cleveland State in the 2008–9 season.

Stevens's star may have ascended to new heights in a 2017 playoff game against the Cleveland Cavaliers. Two days after the Cavs defeated the Celtics by 44 points, Boston rallied from 21 points behind in the third quarter to win on a last-second shot by Bradley. The Celtics' final three baskets resulted from plays designed by their coach.

Following that game, ESPN announcer Kevin Connors remarked, "This guy's a great coach and a lot of times it's hard for the viewer to notice when there's great coaching going on. For me, with Brad Stevens you can see it. You can flat out see the execution."[4]

"Whatever Brad draws up, whatever it is we all believe in it," Bradley said after the Cavs game. "Those are all plays that Brad makes and it's our job to go out and make sure that we make the next right play."[5]

"It's not easy to come up with a great play. I commend Brad because he does a great job night in and night out. He puts us in the right position to succeed," Smart added.[6]

47 | HAYWARD IN HIGH DEMAND

SEVEN YEARS AFTER STEVENS AND Hayward led Butler to the precipice of basketball immortality, Stevens would once again be recruiting Hayward to play for his team.

Both were older, having grown out of their boyish good looks. Both were wiser, having the benefit of experience in the NBA. Both were richer, and Hayward was about to become a lot richer.

Stevens had coached the Boston Celtics to the best record in the NBA East in 2017. Hayward had averaged 21.9 points a game over the long season for the Utah Jazz. As evidence of his value in the clutch, Hayward averaged 24.1 during the 2017 playoffs. He had made the NBA All-Star Game roster, and Stevens had made it as coach of the East.

Hayward was an unrestricted free agent following the 2017 season, meaning he could sign with the highest bidder or with whichever team might want him. The Celtics, said to be one player short of possibly winning the NBA championship, wanted him badly.

Hayward's decision came down to three possible choices. He could remain with the Utah Jazz or move to the Miami Heat or join his former coach and the Celtics. The Celtics took Gordon and his wife, Robyn, to Fenway Park where the scoreboard pointed out the virtues of playing professionally in Boston. On

July 14, 2017, Hayward announced that he would go with the Celtics. According to Dan Forsburg of ESPN he signed a four-year contract for $128 million.

Early in his first regular-season game with the Celtics on October 17, 2017, Hayward suffered a gruesome broken ankle that sidelined him for the rest of the season.

A few days earlier, Mack also signed with a new team, the Orlando Magic. Mack's contract called for him to make $12 million over two years, according to *USAToday*.

48 | "ON THE GROUND FLOOR OF INTEGRATION"

THE EARLY 1950S SAW SOME of Indianapolis's greatest basketball players pass through Butler Fieldhouse. The face of the sport was changing, and those changes were reflected on the Butler campus where Crispus Attucks High was raising the bar to a new level.

Crispus Attucks was one of only three African American schools in the state, and it would soon become the first capital city school to win a state championship. However, not all basketball fans in Indianapolis supported the Tigers. With racial tensions remaining high in the '50s, the team stirred up checkered emotions in the city where neither race was totally ready to accept the other.

Crispus Attucks broke onto the city's sports pages in 1951 when Attucks reached the semifinal game of the State Finals. En route, the Tigers won the sectional, regional, and semistate rounds, all played on Indiana's biggest stage, Butler Fieldhouse. The Tigers were led by six-foot-eight Willie Gardner, one of the greatest players never to play college basketball. The Tigers also had a sophomore forward named Hallie Bryant and a fine center in Bob Jewell.

Attucks was strong again in 1952, but that year Tech broke out of the Indianapolis Sectional and, led by future Butler coach

Joe Sexson, didn't lose until the state's championship game. Individual talent was all over Indianapolis and included Dick Nyers, Bob Springer, Bailey Robertson, and Bailey's still-growing kid brother, Oscar.

Attucks had no home gym, so the bulk of its games were played at Butler. In 1953 Bryant and Bailey Robertson took the Tigers to the semistate where they were upset by Shelbyville.

All over the black sections of Indianapolis talent was developing, especially at Lockefield Gardens where the annual Dust Bowl was contested on the hottest days of summer. The competition was mostly among African Americans, along with a redheaded white guy named Wally Cox and another white kid from out in the county named Ken Pennington.

Cox lived at Seventeenth and College but was born at his grandmother's home at Fourteenth and Stadium Drive, near the old Indianapolis Indians baseball stadium. His grandmother, a product of the times, carried a bias toward the other race until Wally's friends influenced her thoughts.

As Wally said, "I was there when the Ku Klux Klan was still cooking, and I was able to go in there in the black neighborhood. I got along with them because of basketball."[1]

Cox had become close friends with some of the Attucks stars such as Bill Hampton, Bill Scott, Sheddrick Mitchell, Cleveland Spencer, and Bill Brown. "When the first game was over, we'd go right up the street to my house, black guys and Pennington and me, and my mom and grandma would fix a bunch of sandwiches. We'd lay around the backyard relaxing and then we went right back and played another game," Cox said. "Then we'd come back to the house and lay around again.

"The Ku Klux Klan was pretty active in Southern Indiana, and my grandmother had grown up with this prejudicial attitude. The blacks were as prejudiced against whites as the whites were against blacks. When I started playing basketball, my grandmother converted over to accepting the blacks. She found out they were really great guys, and they were welcome to our home, to our food, our bathrooms. This was a great step forward for my family."

Cox said a future Detroit Piston named Shellie McMillon once brought a team to Indianapolis to test the Lockefield Gardens group. "They were going to clean up this tournament. The only problem was that we beat 'em," Cox said.

On one occasion Cox, Pennington, Brown, and a car full of Attucks players were running late for a game in the Mermaid Festival in North Webster, Indiana. "Pennington was driving his big old Pontiac and he was doing ninety miles an hour up Highway 421," Cox recalled. "I'm riding in the back with Brown and Hampton, and we get there just in time. We take a couple of [warmup] shots, and it's time to start. We swept the tournament. We had a hell of a team."

Despite Attucks's success, basketball integration took hold slowly. Cox had no black teammates when he attended Broad Ripple, but when the Rockets won the state in 1980, the team was mostly African American, including the coach.

Integration on college teams was also slow. Of all the fine players at Crispus Attucks, Bryant was the only one who went to Indiana, the 1953 NCAA champion. IU had just integrated in 1947 when Shelbyville's Bill Garrett enrolled, eventually to become an All-American. Garrett was the first black player to regularly start in the Big Ten.

Shelbyville apparently was the only team at any level to start three African Americans when it won the state high school crown in 1947. The Golden Bears, also featuring black players Emerson Johnson and Marshall Murray, upset previously unbeaten Terre Haute's Garfield High and Clyde Lovellette.[2]

"Oscar [Robertson] only lived about a mile from Butler. He lived on Boulevard Place right down the street from Hinkle

Fieldhouse," Cox said. "He was probably close to going to Butler but Cincinnati wanted him and it turned out very well for him."

Butler was only slightly quicker to integrate than IU with former Attucks stars Scott and Mitchell becoming Bulldogs. Cox said that on a road trip to play Michigan the team had to change its hotel and restaurant accommodations because of prejudice.

Cox considers it among his greatest blessings that he got to play with such talented, and likeable, African Americans.

"I was on the ground floor of integration. I couldn't have been born and raised and played ball at a better time," he said.

49 | ARCHEY'S 85 STRAIGHT FREE THROWS

DARNELL ARCHEY IS A NATIVE of New Castle, Indiana, which automatically means he could shoot peas off a tree branch. Seemingly, everybody from New Castle can shoot, beginning with former Indiana All-American Steve Alford.[1]

After Alford and another All-American, Kent Benson, migrated to IU, there seemed to be a pipeline of great shooters coming out of New Castle to fill baskets at Hinkle Fieldhouse. Besides Archey, Miller, Hahn, Stigall, and Chrysler High All-State guard Bruce Horan all wore Butler blue.

Archey was a mere six feet tall and 160 pounds, which scared away many college coaches, but put him fifteen feet from the basket, and he may have been the best marksman in college history. Over a period of twenty-four months, Darnell didn't miss a single free throw in competition. The streak lasted for fifty-seven games against twenty-two different opponents in eleven different arenas (see Table 49.1). Archey made 31 of his NCAA record 85 straight at Hinkle Fieldhouse. From February 15, 2001, until January 18, 2003, he didn't miss. He made them in the NCAA Tournament. He made them in Hawaii. He made them against big schools such as Indiana and against smaller schools such as Lipscomb. He made 11 against Detroit and 2 or less against fifteen teams.

Table 49.1 Archey's Free-Throw Streak, February 15, 2001–January 18, 2003

Date	Opponent	Free Throws
Feb. 15, 2001	Wisconsin-Milwaukee	2–2
Feb. 17, 2001	Wisconsin-Green Bay	1–1
Feb. 22, 2001	Loyola (IL)	2–2
Feb. 24, 2001	Illinois-Chicago	5–5
March 6, 2001	Detroit Mercy	2–2
March 16, 2001	Wake Forest	4–4
March 18, 2001	Arizona	2–2
Dec. 3, 2001	Lipscomb	3–3
Dec. 17, 2001	Mount St. Mary's	2–2
Dec. 28, 2001	Samford	4–4
Dec. 29, 2001	Indiana	2–2
Jan. 17, 2002	Wisconsin-Green Bay	2–2
Jan. 23, 2002	Loyola (IL)	2–2
Feb. 9, 2002	Cleveland State	2–2
Feb. 23, 2002	Illinois-Chicago	3–3
March 14, 2002	Bowling Green	4–4
Dec. 5, 2002	Indiana State	8–8
Dec. 7, 2002	Evansville	6–6
Dec. 10, 2002	Bradley	7–7
Dec. 21, 2002	Saint Louis	2–2
Dec. 28, 2002	Texas-Pan American	2–2
Dec. 29, 2002	Western Kentucky	5–5
Dec. 30, 2002	Hawaii	2–2
Jan. 4, 2003	Illinois-Chicago	3–3
Jan. 11, 2003	Detroit Mercy	6–6
Jan. 16, 2003	Wright State	2–2
Jan. 18, 2003	Youngstown State	1–2

Courtesy of Butler University.

By the time the streak ended, Archey had flown past the old NCAA record of 73 straight set in 2000–01 by Gary Buchanan of Villanova. Darnell finally missed with 3:42 remaining in a Butler victory over Youngstown State.

The new record was actually challenged by Butler's A. J. Graves, who drained 63 in a row during the 2006–07 season.

Graves launched the 2006–07 season by making 91 of his first 92 free-throw attempts. Graves's streak ranks as the fourth longest in NCAA Division I history.

Archey could also fill the basket up from other distances. In his most famous outing, a 79–74 win over Louisville in the 2003 NCAA Tournament in Birmingham, Alabama, he made 8 of his 9 three-point attempts en route to a 26-point game. After the season, he won the Men's Collegiate Three-Point Championship at the Final Four. His playing career ended by touring with the Harlem Globetrotters and an Australian team.

Archey played on three NCAA Tournament teams at Butler and had 217 threes. He had a season free-throw percentage of 97.3 percent and was 95.1 percent over his college career.

Archey spent four years on Butler's staff and is now a member of Matthew Graves's coaching staff at South Alabama. Matthew is a former Butler player (1993–98) and coach (under Lickliter and Stevens), and older brother of A. J.

While growing up, Archey attended Alford's basketball camps and tried to emulate his hero's smooth shooting. While practicing at New Castle High, which has the world's largest high school gym, Darnell once made 96 practice free throws in a row. He would often stay after practice until he had made 25 straight.

Archey also coached five years in high school, including three as head coach at Park Tudor in Indianapolis. One of his players there was future Indiana star Yogi Ferrell. Before coming to Park Tudor, Darnell spent two seasons as head coach at Columbus North. He also spent a season at Carmel High, where he helped tutor future Duke and NBA star Josh McRoberts.

50 | "YOU CAN'T TEACH SHOOTING"

WITH THE UNIVERSITY LOCATED IN the heart of Hoosier Hysteria, Butler's ability to recruit outstanding shooters should not be a surprise. The Bulldogs have enjoyed such marksmen as—just to mention a few—Darrin Fitzgerald, A. J. Graves, Tom Bowman, Rotnei Clarke, Keith Greve, Chad Tucker, Shelvin Mack, Gordon Hayward, Billy Shepherd, Darnell Archey, Darin Archbold, Kellen Dunham, and, perhaps the most colorful of them all, Pete Campbell.

There's a compilation of Campbell's outside shooting on YouTube that will make you wonder if the kid is for real. Standing six feet seven, Campbell played the 2007 and 2008 seasons at Butler after transferring from IPFW.

Johnson was on the IPFW staff for a time and worked with Campbell at the Fort Wayne school. "All I did was stand under the basket and throw it back to him," Butler's former assistant coach said. "I know he was real good at catch and shoot," Johnson added. "I tried to get him to do a lot of things on the move. I tried to wear him down a little bit so he could shoot when he was tired, and we worked on his post game a little bit. He could score and play. It wasn't all three-pointers."

"When people ask who was the best shooter you've seen at Butler, Pete's the name that pops into my mind," said McGrath,

Butler's longtime sports information director. "Any time the ball was in his hands I felt good. I knew if the shot went up it was going in."

Campbell played high school ball at Yorktown, where he was used largely in the pivot and was a three-time All-Hoosier Heritage Conference selection. He was named the Anderson *Herald-Bulletin* Co-Player of the Year in 2003. He averaged 21 points and 8 rebounds as a senior and set a school free-throw percentage record of .892 as a sophomore. He was also a goalkeeper in soccer and a first baseman on the diamond.

Enrolling at IPFW, Campbell redshirted his first season and started seven games his next season while averaging 11 points a game. He gave a hint of the future by scoring 28 points against Kent State.

Transferring to Butler after former Indiana star Dane Fife was named IPFW coach, Campbell became an immediate standout for the Bulldogs. "He was kind of let go from IPFW. I'm not sure exactly what happened, but I'm glad he ended up at Butler. It worked out really well," Johnson said.

Campbell led the Horizon League in three-pointer percentages his first year at Butler and was third in field-goal shooting at .520; he was an even hotter .581 in the conference. He had 14 points in nineteen minutes as the Dawgs almost upset Florida in the NCAA Tournament. Against Old Dominion in the same tournament, he erupted for 9 points in a ninety-one-second span. He enjoyed a 28-point game at Cleveland State in which he hit 6 of 8 threes in the first half.

McGrath said Butler played against Campbell's IPFW team when Pete was a freshman, but added, "He was a center. He had a nice touch, but you didn't see him as a three-point shooter."

"As he got older his body matured a little bit," Johnson said. "I heard he wasn't in shape [during his IPFW days], but you can't teach shooting."

51 | BULLDOGS FIGHT FOR RECOGNITION

IN LATE JANUARY OF THE 2016–17 season, Butler was ranked thirteenth in the AP national basketball poll. Despite a 17–3 record with victories over top-ranked Villanova and four other ranked teams (Arizona, Cincinnati, Indiana, and Xavier), the Bulldogs hadn't made the Top 10 all season.

Seemingly, the Butler program registers on a different scale with writers in the AP poll and coaches in the *USAToday* poll. Since the turn of the century, the Bulldogs' accomplishments have, for the most part, been underappreciated.

Butler did not make the rankings from 1949 until 2002 when it reached a peak of No. 20 late in the season on the heels of a 26–6 record that included thirteen straight victories at the start of the season. That streak featured a win at Purdue and a victory over eventual national runner-up Indiana.

The following season saw the Dawgs ignored in the AP poll and only twenty-first in the coaches' rankings. The latter recognition wasn't awarded until the last poll of the year. Butler finally got some attention during the 2006–07 season when the Dawgs were named over sixteen straight weeks in both polls, yet they never cracked the Top 10 with the AP.

That year Butler went 29–7 with wins over Notre Dame, Indiana, Tennessee, Gonzaga, and Maryland. In 2008 Butler got as high as No. 8 with twenty-six wins and in 2009 didn't hit the Top 10 despite another twenty-six wins. The magical 2010 run with twenty-five straight victories saw the Dawgs fail to reach the Top 10. Their late run to the final game in 2011 wasn't noticed by pollsters, who didn't rank them after the first two weeks of the season.

Butler's move to the Big East received more attention, but its highest ranking over a two-year period through 2015 was ninth. A single loss dropped it nine spots the next week.

Over the years since the Bulldogs lost a heartbreaker to Florida in 2000, confidence in Butler has steadily climbed, yet while everyone acknowledges that the school has a fine program, there has been a reluctance to credit the Bulldogs in the rankings.

Collier agrees that at times the Bulldogs are overlooked: "Yes, and that's probably a good thing from the standpoint of keeping our egos in check," he said. "I don't think we're dismissed or anything, but there's certainly an element of truth in that. Now I hear about people saying we shouldn't be surprised [at the team's lack of a high ranking]."

52 | SIZE DOESN'T MATTER HERE

THERE ARE A COUPLE OF numbers that stand out about Darrin Fitzgerald, who played point guard and shooting guard positions at Butler.

One is his height—five feet nine? Uh, at least some claim he is five-nine.

The other is his point total—2,019—over his four seasons at Butler. That makes him the second highest scorer in Bulldog history to teammate Chad Tucker, who tallied 2,321.

"Talk about a little guy who could shoot from a distance. The three-point rule made him a great player because he shot it a long way," said McGrath. "We listed him at five-eight and that was generous. He probably was closer to five-six and a half, but he was quick, a good athlete."

Fitzgerald's senior season (1986–87) saw him average 26.2 points a game, two points higher than Tucker did that season. However, a redshirt season because of injury provided Tucker four more games to reach his total. In 1987 Fitzgerald had games in which he made 12, 10, and 9 three-pointers against Detroit, Loyola, and Evansville, respectively. His 734 points in '87 ranks second highest in school history, slotting him between Darin Archbold and Billy Shepherd. In the game in which he made 12 threes he also scored 54 points.

Butler won that game against Detroit 88–77 as Darrin made 16 of 30 shots, including 12 of 22 three-pointers. He also made all 10 of his free throws and committed only two turnovers in forty minutes. He carried the load that night because his teammates were only 11 of 29 from the field and 0 for 2 on threes.

Darrin's 158 three-pointers in 1987 marks the all-time season high for a Bulldog, outdistancing the 115 by Clarke. His scoring average of 26.2 as a senior trails only Shepherd's 27.8 in 1970. Darrin's 176 career steals ranks fifth on Butler's list.

The NCAA invoked the three-point shot entering Fitzgerald's senior season, and the Indianapolis Washington product took full advantage of it. In his 54-point game, he posted 34 points in the second half, when he made 7 of 10 three-pointers.

Darrin scored in double figures in all twenty-eight games in 1986–87, including seven games over 30, two over 40, and the 54-pointer. He shot .440 from the field, .776 at the foul line, and .437 on threes. He also had more assists than turnovers and averaged almost four rebounds a game.

53 | HINKLE STARS AS NAVY COACH

AS WORLD WAR II CAST its shadow across the nation, athletes from all sports left to serve their country, and Butler's head coach was no exception.

Hinkle reported to Great Lakes Naval Training Station in Northern Chicago in 1942 and carried the rank of commander by the time of his discharge. Although Tony didn't run into the enemy during his stint in the navy, he did rub elbows with numerous athletes from various levels of different sports. The coach of little Butler University in Indianapolis served as head football coach at Great Lakes with future National Football League coaches Wilber "Weeb" Ewbank, Paul Brown, and Blanton Collier as assistants.

Hinkle also worked with the Great Lakes baseball program, which was under the direction of Hall of Fame catcher Mickey Cochrane. Hinkle was over the football and basketball programs when he was called into his superior's office and told to do one thing: win. The navy considered it important that the naval station win in order to boost morale of sailors stationed there.

Part of the recruiting process was to locate sailors who were good athletes and place them on the Great Lakes teams. The enlisted men were only allowed to play one year before getting new orders. Hinkle's teams played mostly against college teams, and in 1942–43 Great Lakes went 43–3 with losses to Illinois, Northwestern, and Notre Dame.

After the war, *Chicago Tribune* sportswriter Arch Ward, who was the founding force behind baseball's All-Star game, started the All-American pro football league. According to the late *Indianapolis Star* writer Ray Marquette, Paul Brown's Cleveland Browns originated in that league, and Ward wanted Hinkle to coach the team in Chicago. Tony considered it but wanted to return to Butler.

Butler, like many schools, had continued its basketball program throughout the war. Frank "Pop" Hedden had assumed coaching duties until Tony returned to the helm before the 1945–46 season. Over the next four seasons, Butler won 60 of 87 games.

Hinkle would admit that his association with players and coaches at Great Lakes had a positive effect on Butler athletes as well as on his own development.

54 | THE BULLDOGS' FIRST NIT TRIP

BUTLER ENTERED THE 1957–58 SEASON with an all-star lineup but a doughnut hole at center. The backcourt featured former "Mr. Basketball" Bobby Plump and senior Wally Cox, who had led the Bulldogs in scoring as a freshman.[1] Ted Guzek, an All-American and 21-point scorer as a junior, was set at one forward and Keith Greve, one of the school's all-time top scorers, was set at the other. Greve was returning from a stint in the service.

That left the center position without anyone of experience, and that's where Ken Pennington, a sophomore from Warren Central High, entered the picture.

Pennington would become one of the most unlikely pivotmen in Butler history, and one of the best. He was a measly six feet four—he couldn't jump very high, and he couldn't run very fast. Yet, he was as strong as a bull and had a skill that had almost vanished from the college game.

Kenny had a head-and-ball fake that few opposing centers could resist. In the Hoosier Classic victory over Indiana, he faked All-American Archie Dees so thoroughly that Dees's feet were above his head. Many lesser centers were also faked until they fell across Pennington's broad back.

"He'd get guys off their feet and then go underneath them," Cox recalled. "He did not go over them with a jump shot. It was kind of a pivot shot. Pennington had that marvelous move to the right, left, fake, get his man off his feet . . . Kenny was not a high jumper. He couldn't even dunk. Pennington was a little heavier on his feet, had a big butt and, boy, could he move guys around."

"Ken Pennington made the difference at center. It freed up Wally Cox to come back to guard from forward," Plump said. "He could play either position. Wally was a great player. He wasn't as good a scorer as Ted and myself, but we had a great season my senior year. Mr. Hinkle said they didn't have enough basketballs for the four of us."

Greve was as unique a player as Pennington—at least for the late 1950s. Standing only six feet two, Keith never shot a jump shot, but his set shot from great distances seemed to penetrate the smoke-filled caverns high above the floor. Keith totaled 1,400 points over a four-year career that started in 1951 and ended in 1958.

"He played low to the floor. He had a big butt, and he could move guys around rebounding," Cox said. "He was very fundamentally sound. Not a flashy player, but he had a hell of an outside shot."

"Keith came back for his senior year and he made us a much better ball club," Plump said. "He wasn't a big guy, and he wasn't exactly lightning on the floor, but he was a great shooter and a great rebounder. He shot from the side, and the ball would twist and looked like it curved but it went in the basket."

Neither Greve nor Cox shot a jump shot, but their outside shooting complemented Guzek's inside scoring and Plump's drives and midrange jumpers. The Bulldogs were also strengthened when former Crispus Attucks guard Bill Scott transferred in from Franklin.

"He was a great guy. If Wally hadn't been as good as he was, Bill Scott would have been in there. Scott played guard when Guzek was hurt," Plump said. "We had people on the bench that typically would have been starting at other schools."

Plump said Pennington was the only true center he played with at Butler, succeeding Henry Foster for the 1957–58 season. "Henry was our center for two years, and he never had played basketball before," Plump said. "Henry was one of the greatest guys I've ever known. He could jump but couldn't shoot very well. One day he stole the ball and dribbled down the court. He went up to dunk and the ball ended up at midcourt."

Plump, of course, may be the most famous player in Indiana high school history, his legend possibly rising above those of Oscar Robertson, Larry Bird, and the like. His last-second shot had given tiny Milan the 1954 state championship, which he followed up with a stellar career at Butler.

"Plump was a good, good player, but to tell you who the best players were in Butler history—he would be in the top fifteen or twenty," Cox rationalized. "You've got to start with guys like Chad Tucker, and you've got to get Darrin Fitzgerald in there, and you've got guys like [Gordon] Hayward, and don't forget about Buckshot O'Brien, Jimmy Doyle, John Barrowcliff, Keith Greve, Kenny Pennington, Bill Scott. I love Bob. Bobby was a great teammate, but we had a great team that year."

Butler beat Indiana 84–78 and IU went on to win the Big Ten that year. Butler also downed the Hurryin' Hoosiers the next year and in the 1959–60 season lost despite Pennington's 36 points against six-ten Walt Bellamy.

The 1957–58 team was the only team to have five starters average in double figures, Cox noted.

Bill Scott averaged about 30 points as a freshman at Franklin before transferring to Butler. He was the sixth man in 1958 and was Butler's leading scorer the following season.

"Scotty was just a marvelous player," Cox said. "When he would come in he could play forward or he could play guard, but as far as I was concerned one of his best skills was playing the post."

The 1958 Bulldogs posted a 14–9 record and made the school's first postseason appearance in the NIT, played entirely in the old Madison Square Garden. Butler fell there to St. John's in the first round, 76–69, a loss that still grates on some of the Dawgs.

Cox believes Pennington fell victim to a number of bad calls by East Coast officials in that game. In that day and age, before television and improved travel methods made intersectional play commonplace, college basketball in the East was substantially different than in the Midwest.

"I thought he got a raw deal out there at the NIT. They had never seen a pivotman like him out East," Cox said. "He had that fake left, fake right, and he'd get guys off their feet. As the game progressed he got called for a travel, and he got called for a another travel, and he got called for an offensive foul. They had never seen anything like it. He did not have what I would call a sterling game."

Plump agreed with Cox's assessment of the officiating.

"In the NIT tournament they called travel on him so many times. He didn't travel, but they sure as hell called it. Maybe he had one or two travels that whole year, but he probably had three or four in that game," Plump said. "Kenny was unique. The first time I saw him in practice I thought, 'What the hell is this guy doing?' It was so hard to guard him because you really didn't know if he was going to shoot or not. Sometimes he would shoot off the first fake or sometimes he'd fake two or three times. It worked so well."

Cox left the Garden with a bit of a bad taste, having been credited with 19 points by the official scorer. Butler's own scorer had Cox with 21, and it was believed that the official book credited one of Cox's baskets to Guzek. Thus, Cox's career total added up to 999 points, one bucket from breaking the 1,000 mark.

Greve and Pennington had lengthy coaching careers, but Greve, Scott, and Guzek are now deceased. Plump was an

Indianapolis insurance man for years and operates a restaurant called Plump's Last Shot. Pennington's daughter, Jennifer, married former Butler star Tim McRoberts, and their two sons became basketball standouts: Josh McRoberts at Duke and in the NBA and Zach with the Indiana Hoosiers.

55 | BUTLER WINS A PAIR IN ITS FIRST NCAA TOURNAMENT

UNTIL 1962 THE BULLDOGS HAD never been to an NCAA Tournament. They had made the NIT field in both 1958 and '59, advancing to the second round in '59 before losing to Bradley. At the time, being selected for the NIT, held entirely in New York, was almost as great an honor as making it to the NCAA Tournament.

The 1962 NCAA Tournament had only twenty-five teams, forty-three fewer than the expanded field of 2017. The entire attendance at the 1962 tournament was only 177,000, compared with about 70,000 at each of Butler's 2010 Final Four games.

Hinkle's 1962 team may have been his best, posting a 20–5 mark during the regular season. At the time, the Bulldogs played a rugged preconference schedule, and they lost four of their first seven games: to Illinois, Purdue, DePauw, and Michigan State. Their early season wins were also against strong programs: New Mexico State, Michigan, and Bradley.

Butler's lineup that season could probably hold its own against the school's latter-day teams. Its centerpiece was six-foot-six sophomore Jeff Blue, a strong physical presence who could sky. The other major scorers were six-foot-four Tom Bowman, whose outside shooting could be measured in zip codes. The third Butler player to make All-Conference was Gerry Williams, a five-foot-eight will-o'-the-wisp who could dunk, drive, and shoot from outside equally well.

The other regulars were Ken Freeman and Dick Haslam, role players who fit their roles perfectly. Freeman, at six-three, was a starting tight end on the football team and a rebounding and defensive specialist in basketball. Haslam was the captain, a five-nine flash who could hawk the ball on defense and set up the fast break on offense. He started his final 66 games at Butler.

Don Wilson had been the starting center before Blue became eligible, and Larry Shook, Gordon Pope, and Earl Engle were capable off the bench. Engle had been a starting forward in 1959 and returned to the team after two years in the service.

Once the Bulldogs got past the Big Ten portion of their schedule, they burped only once during the rest of the regular season, a conference loss at Valparaiso. They won their next thirteen, including two victories over archrival Evansville, and knocked off Notre Dame twice while winning seventeen of eighteen.

Bowman, a junior from Martinsville, Indiana, led the team in scoring at 18.4 points a game, hitting 48 percent of his mostly long shots. Blue and Williams each averaged 15.9, and Blue shot above 50 percent.

The ICC never enjoyed automatic entry into the national tournament, but Butler's season was hard to ignore, and the Bulldogs were paired against Bowling Green in Lexington, Kentucky. They were among six teams in the Mideast Region, the others being Kentucky, Ohio State, Detroit, and Western Kentucky.

Bowling Green (with a regular season record of 18–2) was led by future NBA star Nate Thurmond. After the selection was announced, Hinkle told the *Indianapolis News*, "I don't know much about them except that they have a seven-footer. We'll chop him down."[1]

Thurmond wasn't flattened, but his 21 points weren't enough to save the Falcons from their third loss, 56–55. Bowman scored 18, Blue 16, and Williams 13 to advance the Bulldogs to the second round.

"The kids did just about everything they were supposed to do," Hinkle told the *Indianapolis Star.* "They had the patience to keep things slowed down and work for the stuff we thought would work against Bowling Green."[2]

Bowling Green had been consistently ranked among the nation's top 10 teams all season. Bowling Green's 55 points was its lowest total of the season. Butler led by 3 points at halftime and, helped by Blue's 12 rebounds, outnumbered the Falcons on the boards.

In the mid-twentieth century, one of the fallacies of the NCAA Tournament remained in effect. The pairings usually saw teams play close to their campuses, and home-court advantages often existed. For instance, Kentucky won the national title in 1958 by winning all four games in Kentucky, two on its home court in Lexington and two in Louisville. It could also have gotten a break in 1962 because the Wildcats, after getting a first-round bye, would have played the Final Four in Louisville had they won in Iowa City.

That first game was to be against Butler, which was praised by Kentucky coach Adolph Rupp after it beat Bowling Green. The Wildcats were undoubtedly looking ahead to a possible match against Ohio State, the NCAA champion in 1960 and runner-up in 1961. The Buckeyes were led by Jerry Lucas and John Havlicek and had a reserve forward named Bob Knight. But first Kentucky would have to worry about Butler.

On entering the 1962 NCAA Tournament, Kentucky had already won four national championships and was generally considered the top program in the nation. The Wildcats were the scourge of the Southeastern Conference and had gone 22–2 that season, losing only to Southern California, 79–77, and Mississippi State, 49–44. The not yet integrated Wildcats were led by All-American Cotton Nash and had a roster with thirteen in-state players. They weren't tall with the six-five Nash their biggest starter. However, Kentucky had two six-foot guards matched against Butler's Haslam at five-nine and Williams at five-eight.

Ohio State, which would drop the title game to Cincinnati for the second straight season, was ranked No. 1 with Kentucky No. 3 entering the games at Iowa City. But, despite its 21–5 record, Butler hadn't gotten a sniff in the polls all season.

The Bulldogs hadn't played in nineteen days going into the Bowling Green game because their home court had been laid aside for Indiana's high school tournament. Butler proved its worth by trailing Kentucky only 37–36 at halftime as Blue had 14 points and 6 rebounds. Kentucky never led by more than 6 points in the first half but owned a 20–14 rebounding advantage. Butler took the lead on Bowman's jumper shortly after play resumed. Butler's shooting then fell off until the Wildcats moved ahead 64–49 with 6:50 remaining. Over the first thirteen minutes of the second half, the Bulldogs made only 4 of 23 shots. Williams led Butler with 20 points, and Blue added 19 while Billy Joe Pursiful and Nash combined for 49 Kentucky points.

Thus, the Kentucky-Ohio State matchup became a reality and the Buckeyes triumphed, 74–64.

Butler didn't have to go home because each regional and the Final Four had a consolation game. Western Kentucky, a 93–73 loser to the Buckeyes, would meet the Bulldogs to vie for third place. The Hilltoppers, coached by Ed Diddle and led by future pro Darel Carrier and Bobby Rascoe, matched Butler basket for basket until the Bulldogs escaped with an 87–86 victory in overtime.

Blue, Bowman, and Williams returned the following season, but the Bulldogs struggled some without Freeman and Haslam and finished with a 15–10 record. Butler beat only Michigan in its first six games but won ten of its last eleven.

56 | YOU WANT TO COME TO BUTLER, KID?

HINKLE WAS NEVER A CANDIDATE for one of those exposés on coaches who violate recruiting rules. His attempts to get players to come to Butler were low-key—to say the least.

Cox, who stood six feet four and starred at Indianapolis Broad Ripple High, had been offered a full scholarship to attend the University of Miami. However, since Butler would soon be able to offer grants-in-aid, Hinkle paid a visit to Cox's home. It turned out to be mostly a social call.

"Hinkle was looking for a tall guard to play alongside this little guy named Plump," Cox recalled. "He spent three minutes talking about basketball and about forty-five minutes talking with my dad about hunting, fishing, and farming. That was it. Give him a call if I was interested. He knows I'm going to Miami, but if I'm interested in Butler—I'd like to have you. You can call me.

"And I was sitting there thinking, 'Hell, maybe he doesn't want me coming to Butler. Maybe he and my dad are just becoming friends.'"

Plump, the small-town boy from Milan, wasn't pushed hard, either. Hinkle sent him a handwritten letter that read:

Dear Bob:

First, may I congratulate you and your teammates on winning the IHSAA [Indiana High School Athletic Association] championship. I probably got as big a kick out of it as you boys did.

Bob, I want you to come to Butler. We have a small school and I know you will be satisfied here. We have a bunch of boys. Also, I have a man who has taken an interest in you and wants to help you through school financially. Sometime when you get some time I want you to come up. I want to introduce you to the man and give you an application for admissions filled out.

Many schools probably will be after you. But just make up your mind to be with us. You can't go wrong. When can you come up?

Sincerely,

Tony Hinkle

P.S.: If any of the other boys want to come with you bring them along.[1]

Plump said Hinkle never visited his home in Pierceville, and Tony was right, many other schools did want Plump.

"I turned down IU, Purdue, Michigan State, Cincinnati, Tennessee, and thirty-five other colleges," Plump said.

Hinkle's letter referred to a man who would help Bobby financially, and without his help Plump said he couldn't have attended Butler.

"I met that man, an investment man, at the Sigma Chi house. Mr. Hinkle said I could have my choice of jobs. I swept the floor, which got me into the state tournament every year."

When grants-in-aid became available a year later, they became his savior.

"My first year all of my expenses were paid. My fraternity dues were paid. My long distance calls were paid," he said.

Plump made and received lots of long distance phone calls from his future wife, Janine, who was in school at Hanover. When Bobby told Hinkle she was moving to Indianapolis with marriage in the works, the coach replied, "Thank goodness Hanover came to Butler. I'm tired of those phone bills."

Cox revealed how he took a Southport High guard named Jimmy Holt on a visit to Hinkle's office.

"Jimmy was an average player at Southport for an old Butler man named Blackie Braden," Cox said. "I had warned Jimmy not to expect a hard sales pitch. 'He will probably just say what a nice school Butler is and talk about having a good school of education,'" Wally told Holt.

"He came and sat down and Mr. Hinkle started talking to him: 'Nice to know you, kid. I understand you're from Southport and Butler's got some teachers and coaches there. This would be a good place for you to think about. If you'd like to come out here, give me a call and we'll work something up.'

"His recruiting of Jimmy Holt lasted from two to three minutes," Cox recalled.

For the most part Hinkle didn't have to be a great recruiter. Perhaps half the high school coaches in central Indiana were Hinkle disciples. Most of them ran what was known as the Hinkle System, and all their players were familiar with Hinkle's simple style of offense. The late Norm Ellenberger, a three-sport star at Butler in the 1950s, once told how coach after coach would bring a prospect into Tony's office and he would hear the same soft sell that Holt had received. Often they would wind up in a Butler uniform.

The Hinkle System was an offense often called Hinkle's Fifth Way, a style that kept the floor balanced and provided options at every turn. "Someone came along and called it the motion offense. They wanted their own name on it, but it's the same thing," Cox said. "Hinkle was a master at simplifying things."

57 | IU RECRUITS PLUMP AGGRESSIVELY

AT THE TIME PLUMP LED Milan to its historic victory in the state tournament, Indiana University was atop the college basketball world. IU won the NCCA championship in 1953 and, with the same starting lineup, was ranked No. 1 the following season.

"I was down at IU four different times," Plump said. "Purdue? I only went there once. I really didn't like the campus, and for some reason didn't like Purdue. I liked IU but it was too big for me. IU put a rush on me; they were great.

"This isn't the reason I didn't go there, but when I talked to Branch McCracken, Bobby Leonard had just graduated, and he had a two-handed set shot." According to Plump, the IU coach said, "We're got a good group coming in, and I'd like you to learn the two-handed set shot to replace Bobby Leonard."

"I'd never shot a two-handed set shot in my life. I either shot a one-handed push shot or a jump shot," Plump said. The jump shot as we know it now was in its infancy in the 1950s. "I was probably the only true jump shooter in the 1954 tournament. [Teammate Ray] Craft jumped and shot but Ray didn't have a jump shot. I don't think Muncie had any. I don't think [Terre Haute] Gerstmeyer had any," said Plump, referring to Milan's opponents in the state finals.

"[IU player] Don Schlundt wrote me two letters, one about six pages long. The players did much of the recruiting then. I just thought IU was too big; I kept going back to Butler. I didn't want to go out of state, but if Michigan State had been in Indiana that probably would have been where I would have gone.

"I was going to coach and teach. I wasn't going to teach and coach. In addition, I knew the Hinkle System because it was used at Milan, and I wouldn't have to learn a new system."

58 | FUN DAYS IN THE ICC

THROUGHOUT ITS HISTORY, BUTLER HAS been a member of six conferences, beginning with the Missouri Valley in 1932 and culminating with its move to the Big East in 2013. In between were the Mid-American, Indiana Collegiate, Midwestern City (later renamed the Horizon League), and A-10.

The Big East has taken the Bulldogs to new heights, leading to almost every game being televised and drawing packed houses to Hinkle Fieldhouse. Yet, when it comes to big rivalries and backyard squabbles, the ICC may have been the most fun.

The ICC was a bus league with most of its members located within two or three hours of each other. Between 1952 and 1978, the Bulldogs won ten ICC championships and constantly had a bull's-eye on their backs.

Butler was the biggest rival for all the ICC teams, which included Ball State, Indiana State, Valparaiso, Evansville, DePauw, and St. Joseph's. Founded in 1951, the ICC was an offshoot of the Indiana Intercollegiate Conference. Butler's schedule in the 1950s and '60s was more glamorous than its ICC rivals' because the Bulldogs played multiple Big Ten teams in December, even drawing some of that league's teams into the fieldhouse.

"The reason we were able to beat a lot of Big Ten teams is we were stronger fundamentally," Plump said.

When the ICC schedule began in January, Butler found its league opponents more than formidable. "Evansville was always tough. One year we beat DePauw twice and those were the only two they lost," Plump said. "Mr. Hinkle had a flaw, and that's the only one I know of. He hated zone defenses and wouldn't play a zone. He had no idea how to defeat a zone defense."

St. Joseph College, which no longer exists, played a 1-3-1 zone defense against the Bulldogs, and it gave them fits. "We probably just broke even with them," Plump said. "All the rest of the league we could handle except for St. Joe and that damn zone. DePauw played a zone but it wasn't the 1-3-1. They played a 2-1-2 and we could beat them. St. Joe had a guard by the name of Dan Rogovich, who was a hell of a player.

"We always had a problem with Evansville down there. We beat them 101–76 when I was a senior, in which I set a single-game record. [Plump's 41 points included a still-standing Butler record 17 of 17 at the foul line.] Then, we went to Evansville and got beat in a double overtime."

Evansville was a five-time champion in the NCAA College Division, and the Purple Aces were Butler's biggest rival during that stretch. The Aces beat the Bulldogs twice in 1951, but the Bulldogs turned the tables on them with two victories in each of the next two years. The teams split two games in 1954 and '55.

"We'd come out of the Evansville game and we'd have scratches on our arms, our legs. They were tougher than hell. Arad McCutchan did a great job with them," Plump said.

Led by Coach McCutchan, the Aces were loaded in the 1960s with future NBA star Jerry Sloan and Madison, Indiana, products Larry Humes and Buster Briley. Still, Hinkle's 1962 team beat them twice en route to a 22–6 record.

If nothing else, the Purple Aces were colorful. McCutchan dressed them in orange uniforms, and while in huddles the reserves wore multicolored robes that reached the floor.

Like Butler, Evansville had a large arena, but St. Joseph's, Valparaiso, DePauw, and Ball State played in cozy gyms where the students were almost on top of the floor. Thus, road games were major challenges for the Bulldogs. In 1958 St. Joe edged Butler's NIT team 64–62 in Rensselaer.

"The last game of my senior year we played DePauw at Butler Fieldhouse," Cox recounted. "Fortunately, we didn't play at their place. It stunk. Their gym was old and crappy. You didn't have much room to take the ball out of bounds. I tried to take the ball out of bounds once and there was a kid there with his knees out. I know he did it on purpose."

Cox remembered playing at Illinois and getting kicked in the rear while taking the ball out of bounds. It could have been worse. Indiana player Charlie Meyer took it out of bounds in Illinois's old Huff Gym and got burned in the leg by a cigarette.[1]

"A lot of places had scrubby gyms," Cox said.

Plump wasn't certain DePauw's gym was regulation length. "It didn't seem like it," he said. "Notre Dame was the same way. At Notre Dame you would take the ball out of bounds and someone would pinch you. The ICC was a great league. It was good for Indiana and it was good in the era that we were playing in."

It was also a low-budget conference. After the game, teams would eat their meals on the bus. "We'd stop where some of Mr. Hinkle's former players would have a place, whether it was a pharmacy or whatever. We'd get a sandwich, milk in those little cardboard things, and maybe an apple," Plump said, laughing.

There was plenty of talent in the ICC, where smallish guards flourished but tall centers were rare. Ball State's Ed Butler was an exceptional talent who dueled with Butler's Jeff Blue near the basket. Long before Larry Bird, Indiana State featured Jerry Newsom and Butch Wade, two strong players from Columbus, Indiana, and St. Joseph's had smallish guards Rogovich and

Bobby Williams, whose quickness frustrated taller opponents. Evansville's Don Buse became an NBA player.

Bobby Williams was a product of Indianapolis Shortridge whose younger brother Gerry was a star on Butler's 1962 NCAA team. Bobby was nicknamed "Biscuit," Gerry was "Muffin," and a third little brother was "Crumb."

By the late 1960s, the ICC was on its last legs and didn't even have a commissioner. Ball State and Indiana State, the two state-supported universities in the conference, were ready for bigger surroundings, and the Sycamores responded by switching to the MVC. Ball State moved over to the MAC. The ICC disbanded in 1979.

Before its demise, the ICC was a haven for veteran coaches. Besides Hinkle and McCutchan, Gene Bartow was at Valparaiso, Elmer McCall at DePauw, and Duane Klueh at Indiana State. Well-known basketball officials Ted Hillary and Steve Welmer played at St. Joseph's and Evansville, respectively.

59 | PLUMP IS SHY OFF THE COURT

PLUMP HAS DONE AN INORDINATE amount of interviews and countless speeches since 1954, but off the basketball court he claims that putting himself on display wasn't a natural thing.

"I can't overemphasize this: I was shy and bashful in high school. People don't believe that now, but I was," Plump said. "People at Butler thought I was stuck up. I didn't go to the C-Club [a campus hangout] because I didn't know how to talk with girls."

Plump reasoned that anyone from Indianapolis or other big cities had to be smarter than he was. "After giving speeches for twenty years, I finally figured out that people are just people."

Plump was raised in Pierceville, a town of 75 people dwarfed by Milan's population of 1,100. Milan had a thousand-seat gym that was sold out for the season.

The former Milan High star said that he never tires of the interviews, which were difficult at first because of his shyness. "It's a unique honor because I was such a shy, bashful guy in high school. I couldn't talk with anybody. I was embarrassed to answer questions in class," he said. "With all the hoopla, they asked me to give speeches and the word 'no' wasn't in my vocabulary, so I said 'yes.'"

The former Butler guard, now in his 80s, may have done as many media interviews as anyone in the state. "It's just nice to be remembered. I think it's a privilege; it's an honor," he said.

One of Plump's most memorable speeches brought him face to face with a man who had a major impact on his life years earlier.

Milan used a double overtime and a timekeeping glitch to beat Morton Memorial in the 1953 Rushville regional. The Indians trailed by 9 points with 48 seconds to play but rallied to force overtime on Ray Craft's basket at the buzzer. However, a major controversy erupted when it was learned that a timekeeping error had occurred and the game clock wasn't turned on following a timeout, meaning that Milan had benefited from extra time.

"I gave a speech at a Sigma Chi luncheon thirty years ago, and I told that story and after the speech a man came up and said, 'I'm the timer,'" Plump recounted.

Milan went on to reach the state finals in both 1953 and '54.

60 | DOWN GOES MICHIGAN

CHRISTMAS OF 1965 WAS APPROACHING and the Grinch was on Butler's doorstep. The Bulldogs had started the season with five losses in their first six games. The win was a two-pointer over Southern California, followed by a one-point loss to visiting Ohio State. Then came successive road losses to Michigan State, Purdue, and Bradley.

Hinkle was pursuing his five hundredth victory throughout the losing streak and finally reached the milestone with the 76–70 win over the Sycamores in Indianapolis. But win number 501 promised to be a tough one with third-ranked Michigan coming into the fieldhouse on December 22.

By many parameters, Michigan may have been the best team in the nation. Coach Dave Strack, a graduate of Indianapolis Shortridge, had a lineup that was deemed impossible for Butler to match up against. It was led by six-foot-six All-American Cazzie Russell, who was joined by six-ten Craig Dill, six-four John Clawson, and six-footer John Thompson. Oliver Darden, a six-seven Adonis-type forward, missed the game with a virus.

Butler's starting guards were five-ten Larry Shade and six-footer Jim Petty, both of whom would be instrumental in Butler's stunning 79–64 win.

The one thing in Butler's favor was that one night earlier the Wolverines had lost to No. 1 Duke 100–93 in overtime. Michigan had hoped a win in that game would boost the Wolverines up in the rankings. The Blue Devils had trailed by 10 points before closing with a 15–3 run to take the lead with 25 seconds left in regulation. Clawson then sent the game into overtime with a basket at the buzzer.

Tired or not, the Wolverines were blitzed by Butler, which took a 41–29 lead at halftime.

Petty's guarding of Russell was one of the greatest defensive efforts in Butler history. The slender guard stuck with the All-American like sweat on his back. Everywhere Cazzie turned, Petty was as close as his belt buckle. Russell finished with 22 points but scored 6 of them in the final 58 seconds of the first half when Petty sat down with three fouls.

Shade sparkled throughout, dashing inside and draining outside jump shots while scoring 16 points and pulling down 6 rebounds. Center Ed Schilling successfully battled the Wolverines inside while scoring 26 points and snatching 13 rebounds.

Butler's first half saw the Bulldogs approach a 20-point lead, to the delight of 9,100 fans. The Bulldogs made 31 of 53 shots. Lon Showley and Ron Salatich completed Butler's lineup, and both scored in double figures. Salatich also claimed 11 rebounds as Butler won the boards, 41–33.

61 | "A TRUCK AND A VW BEETLE—NO MATCH"

TED GUZEK HAD BODY MOVES that chipmunks have yet to equal. He could dart in any direction, shoot the basketball with either hand, and score points in bunches. He was a Helms All-American as a junior, and if he had stood six feet eight instead of six-four, his name would be the stuff of legends.

Guzek scored 1,311 points in four years at forward. He wasn't that great an outside shooter, but from midrange or closer he was dynamite. He played in an all-star lineup that also featured Plump, Greve, Cox, and Pennington in 1957–58.

As a junior he nailed a last-second shot to give the Bulldogs an 86–84 victory over Notre Dame in South Bend. He also scored 38 points that night and was supported by Plump's 32 points. As a sophomore Guzek scored 37 points in a 81–74 triumph over the Fighting Irish in Indianapolis. Ted's best game was on December 15, 1958, when he made 13 out of 13 shots taken against Michigan.

"He could shoot with either hand," Cox said. "A lot of people wondered if he was left-handed because he broke his wrist in high school and he learned to play with his left hand a lot. So, when he came to Butler that was why he was so good. He was right-handed, but he was really good with his left hand."

Added Plump, "Sometimes he would shoot off the wrong foot. It was hard to defend that. He could hit a hook shot. He could drive either way. He had a great junior year and would have had a great senior year but he hurt his ankle."

Guzek averaged 21.3 points as a junior, the season he was named All-American. His average fell off to 11.9 as a senior when he missed five games with an ankle injury, but he still shot 54 percent on the season. Punished by his inside scoring, opponents also attempted to curtail him by playing a lot of zone his senior year. That helped outside shooters Greve and Cox become more prolific.

Guzek was a product of Hammond Morton High, and his brother, Bob, was a former Major League pitcher with the Chicago White Sox and Oakland Athletics.

Ted became an educator on the south side of Indianapolis after his graduation. Guzek and Cox remained close, and after several years in the insurance business, Cox also went into teaching and coaching in the same school district as Guzek.

"I met my wife at his wedding," Cox said. "Ted and his wife, Peggy Kritch, and my wife were best friends. It was in 1972 and he had taught for thirteen or fourteen years at Southport in the junior high programs. He got the appointment as the principal of Southport Middle School.

"That summer he and Peggy and another couple named Shaner were on a scavenger hunt for a church down there. Ted was driving his Volkswagen Bug, his wife was in the front seat, and the Shaners were in the back seat. They were going across Sumner Avenue from Meridian Street over to Bluff Road. There is some kind of rise and before you get there, [there] is a left turn into an addition.

"Ted made a left turn in front of a truck. He turned into that truck's direction. It smashed his car and killed him instantly. It killed the Shaners instantly, and Peggy was in a coma for three or four years. She wilted away to nothing before she died. She was a beautiful lady.

"Unfortunately, Ted was driving a small car. It was no match, a truck and a VW Beetle—no match."

62 | HINKLE'S CRITICISM IS SUBTLE

TONY WASN'T ONE TO SCREAM at a player or grab him by the jersey. Hinkle usually got his criticism across to players using low-key methods.

Butler was playing Indiana State when the Sycamores' Arley Andrews fouled out. Plump, who had roomed with Andrews at a high school All-Star game, went over to the Indiana State bench and shook Arley's hand.

Hinkle didn't say a word, but after the game the players saw his writing on a blackboard: "It is not necessary to shake the hand of a person who fouls out when they go to the bench."

"He never talked to me, never said anything, but I got the point," Plump said. "He was such a unique individual and got his points across in such a way that you weren't upset with him, and you knew that it was something that was going to help you."

Plump recalled the coach admonishing Guzek for his defense.

"At the end of our junior year, Mr. Hinkle called us all together and he said, 'Guzek, you see that post there?'

'Yeah, Mr. Hinkle,' Ted replied.

'I want you this summer to guard that and if it doesn't get around you, maybe you can play next year,' Hinkle said."

Plump said teammate Cox didn't have a jump shot, and when he attempted one in practice the coach stopped play.

"He tried to shoot a jump shot, and Mr. Hinkle blew the whistle.

'Wally, I'm going to show what you look like,'" the veteran coach said.

"Mr. Hinkle came out and jumped up, threw his legs back and threw the ball, and he said, 'Don't do that anymore,'" Plump recalled.

Plump said the Hall of Fame coach might max out emotionally when an official made a call that wasn't in sync with the rulebook.

"He knew the rules inside and out, and if an official made a call that he thought was against the rules, the only thing he'd say was, 'You jackass!' I don't know if he said it loud enough for the officials to hear, but we could hear it," Plump said. "'Jackass.' If he expressed himself, and he didn't do that very often, that's what he would say."

63 | BILLY SHEPHERD, SMALL BUT MIGHTY

BEING NAMED INDIANA'S MR. BASKETBALL is one of the top awards a Hoosier high school player can receive. For Butler University, recruiting a Mr. Basketball can be a formidable task.

Since the honor began in 1939, only two Mr. Basketballs from the state went on to play at Butler. The first was Plump, perhaps the state's largest basketball legend, renown for making the shot that gave tiny Milan the 1954 state championship. The second was Billy Shepherd, a legend in his own right and a scoring machine both at Carmel High School and Butler. Despite playing only three seasons for the Bulldogs, Shepherd ranks eighth in school history with 1,733 career points. For his sixty-six games, Billy averaged 26.3 points, which is the highest scoring average in school history.

Shepherd's best year was as a sophomore in 1969–70 when he scored 27.8 points a game.

(Plump played four seasons and averaged 16.4 points for eighty-eight games.)

Shepherd came from a basketball family that included younger brother Dave, who was Mr. Basketball in 1970. They played at Carmel for their father, Bill Sr., who was an All-Star player at tiny Hope High School and lettered from 1947 to 1949 at Butler.

Billy produced 2,465 points at Carmel while averaging 32 points over his final two seasons. He had a single game of 70 points.

His father led Hope to its only sectional and regional championships in 1945. Bill Sr. coached Carmel to the state's runner-up position in the 1970 IHSAA championship and directed the Greyhounds to fifty straight wins from 1967 to 1970. Dave played at Indiana until transferring to Mississippi.

Billy stood only five feet ten and played in the American Basketball Association (ABA) from 1972 through 1975. He started his pro career with the Virginia Squires and also played for the San Diego Conquistadors and Memphis Sounds. Billy averaged 5.7 points as a pro and led the ABA in 1974–75 with a three-point shooting percentage of .420.

64 | BEVO FRANCIS PLAYED HERE—ONCE

WHEN OLD-TIMERS TALK ABOUT THE legendary figures who have played in Hinkle Fieldhouse, the list begins with Oscar Robertson and ends with Clarence "Bevo" Francis.

Francis played one game at what was then Butler Fieldhouse and scored 48 points. Compared with his average game, that may have been an off night for Bevo. Nevertheless, that was the scoring record at the old barn for seventeen years, until Austin Carr hit 50 for Notre Dame in Hinkle's last game as coach.

Francis was an Ohio farm boy who stood six feet nine and starred at tiny Rio Grande College in Ohio in the 1950s. He performed outrageous feats, especially when he scored 116 points in a game against Ashland Junior College during the 1953–54 season. The following season he scored 113 against Hillsdale College. Bevo—and the country-boy nickname only added to his mystique—had a two-year career in which he exceeded 80 points four times and 64 points nine times.

Not surprisingly, countless people insisted Francis's point totals shouldn't be taken seriously. Coached by the controversial Newt Oliver, whose self-serving style helped publicize Bevo nationwide, Francis averaged 48.3 points in 1952–53. He actually averaged 50, but the NCAA refused to count games against junior colleges, which included the 116-point outburst but not the 113-pointer.

Oliver set up a schedule for the next season that included a few larger basketball schools in an attempt to give Francis an opportunity to prove his worth. One of those was a game at Butler, in which Bevo's 48 points helped Rio Grande to a 81–68 victory. Butler's lineup that night included diminutive guard Jim Crosley and Norm Ellenberger, who would become a legendary coach at New Mexico and later was an assistant under Bob Knight at Indiana.

Francis played only one season in high school, where Oliver was his coach, and only two years at Rio Grande, which had only ninety-two students at the time. He was reportedly an outstanding outside shooter, but his 116-point game saw teammates constantly feed him the ball, leading to a final score of 150–85. The season he played Butler saw him average 46.5 points.

That Butler team finished with a 13–12 record but played a killer schedule in which it opened the season with six straight games against Big Ten opponents: Wisconsin, Ohio State, Illinois, Indiana, Purdue, and Michigan.

Francis died in 2015 at age 82.[1]

65 | TONY'S LAST GAME

ON ONE PARTICULAR NIGHT, WHEN the veteran coach walked up the ramp approaching the cavernous center of Hinkle Fieldhouse, he found himself the center of attention, exactly what he had tried to avoid during most of his forty-one years as Butler's basketball coach.

One source estimated the overflow crowd in the fieldhouse at seventeen thousand, a couple of thousand more people than the old building had seats. Many of the seats were filled by celebrities, including politicians, Indiana Pacers, coaches, and former players. The 70-year-old coach always entered the court from the northeast passage, but this night Hinkle took a less conspicuous route and suddenly arrived at the Butler bench before most of the fans had spotted him.

"I swear he tried to sneak in," *Indianapolis Star* columnist Bob Collins wrote the next day.[1]

It was February 23, 1970, and Tony's Bulldogs were about to meet Notre Dame in what would be Hinkle's last game.

Mr. Hinkle, as he was known to many who considered him more than a coach, had reached Butler's mandatory retirement age. For a time his backers had tried to circumvent that rule and determine him to be a part-time employee. But serving as athletic director and head coach of the basketball, football, and baseball teams didn't fit the description of a part-time job.

For years the Indiana high school landscape had been flooded with coaches who had learned the game from Hinkle. Tony had developed an offense known as the Hinkle System, and it seemed like half the high schools in the state used it. Many times a high school coach would bring one of his top players into Hinkle's office, where the old coach would greet the recruit but never fawn over him.

In 1970 it was hard to imagine Butler without Hinkle. He *was* Butler; together they were like peanut butter and chocolate. Because opposing coaches had so much respect for him, the Bulldogs were able to schedule home games against some of the best teams in the land: John Wooden's UCLA Bruins, Ohio State with John Havlicek and Jerry Lucas, Michigan with Cazzie Russell, and Michigan State with John "Jumpin' Johnny" Green. They all played on Butler's court, and sometimes they left with their tails between their legs.

In those days Butler played Notre Dame twice a year, and Hinkle was so respected in South Bend that the Fighting Irish gave him a free trip to Hawaii at that night's ceremonies. Tony received a telegram of congratulations from the White House, proclamations from the governor of Indiana and the mayor of Indianapolis, and numerous standing ovations from his fans. The man who had coached 560 collegiate victories explained to the throng why all of them came from Butler instead of some pressure-packed program in another part of the land.

"Let's be happy. I'm not ready to roll over and drop dead yet," he said to the crowd. "I sincerely hope I've contributed as much to the people of Indiana, the citizens of Indianapolis and the beloved people of Butler as they have to me."

And then it was time for basketball, the real reason Tony had come to the fieldhouse that night. What the capacity crowd saw was as unlike a Hinkle-coached game as anyone could imagine. The defense-oriented, wait-for-a-good-shot Bulldogs were outpointed 121–114.

As the massive crowd cheered the Bulldogs on, the Fighting Irish proved unstoppable although Butler's offense was almost as potent. If Hinkle mentioned playing better defense in his huddles, it was an admonition that didn't stick.

Austin Carr, Notre Dame's flashy All-American guard, erupted for 50 points, which broke the house record of 48 set by Rio Grande's Bevo Francis. Carr made 22 of 44 shots while teammate Collis Jones hit 18 of 32 for 40 points. The Fighting Irish launched an unlikely 106 shots in the game and made 53 of them. At halftime they led 63–60.

Jones wasn't even supposed to start, but teammate Sid Catlett missed the team bus and didn't even play.

The Bulldogs made only nine turnovers and never fell off the pace as sophomore Billy Shepherd scored 38 and Dave Bennett contributed 30. Shepherd, who remains the eighth-best scorer in the school's history, averaged 31 points over his final fifteen games that season. The Bulldogs finished with a 15–11 record in 1970. Others on that team included Steve Norris, Doug Ferguson, Floyd Garrott, John Marsh, Joe Pearson, Larry Radecki, Bob Schroeder, and John Seal.

66 | GETTING NOTICED BY THE OLD COACH

SHORTLY AFTER COLLIER BECAME BUTLER'S coach, he often found Hall of Fame mentor Hinkle hanging around the fieldhouse. It was always Tony's second home, and he still had an office there.

"When I was a student there, Mr. Hinkle would hold court every day down by the equipment cage with his buddies. There would always be a plume of smoke back in those days—they were all smoking back in the '70s," Collier recalled. "Equipment manager Charlie McElfresh, an Irishman who was a riot . . . big bark, no bite . . . would be there and they would all hold court. Seeing how they appreciated each other was a very cool thing.

"Mr. Hinkle would come to practice every day. We'd come out on the floor and he'd be there. When I became the coach he was still there. He didn't see so well then and he was a lot slower, but he was home. He was 89 then and still coming to the fieldhouses. I'm thinking this guy is a legend; he's forgotten more about basketball than I know."

Collier asked the venerable coach to speak to his team, and Hinkle asked what he should talk about. "*You* want *me* to tell you what to talk about?" Collier thought.

Some joked that in Tony's forty-one years as coach he never learned anyone's name. He either referred to a player as "kid" or called him by the name of his hometown. Such was the case of veteran Jody Littrell, a Columbus East product that Collier said was one of the best players on the team.

"So, [Hinkle] comes in and he's telling them how proud they should be to wear that jersey, and what that jersey should mean to them and so forth, and then he turns to one of our seniors, Jody Littrell, and says, 'You, Columbus, I've been watching you guys for four years and you haven't played defense yet.'

All the other guys fell on the floor laughing."

67 | BUCKSHOT IS A GOOD SHOT

RALPH "BUCKSHOT" O'BRIEN WAS THE last Butler man to play in the NBA until Hayward joined the Utah Jazz fifty years later. A Bulldog from 1947 to 1950, this five-foot-nine player averaged 18 points a game as a senior during a time when scoring was lower.

Buckshot was an All-American in 1949 and '50 and played in the East-West All-Star game of 1950. Academically, he was among the top 10 in his class.

O'Brien played four seasons with the NBA's Indianapolis Olympians and then became an insurance man who sold at least a million dollars in insurance for many years. That made him a member of the prestigious Million Dollar Round Table. In 1975 O'Brien was awarded the NCAA's Silver Anniversary Medal.

At Butler, O'Brien was his team's MVP his last three seasons as well as the MAC's MVP for three seasons. He was the first player to score 1,000 points for the Bulldogs. Most important to O'Brien, he helped Butler to a 60–12 record over his four seasons.

In 1947 he helped Butler win the first Hoosier Classic with victories over Purdue and Indiana. O'Brien's teammates in 1949 included Jim Doyle, Bill Shepherd, Charlie Maas, and Marvin Wood. Wood later coached Milan to the 1954 state championship, and Maas was a longtime coach at Tech. Shepherd is the father of 1970s Butler star Billy Shepherd.

At five-nine, Buckshot was an unlikely professional player, yet he averaged 7 points a game for the Olympians, who played their home games in Butler Fieldhouse. Founded in 1949, the Olympians consisted largely of former University of Kentucky stars such as Ralph Beard, Alex Groza, Cliff Barker, and Wallace "Wah Wah" Jones. However, Beard and Groza were suspended for life from the NBA after being implicated in a massive point-shaving scheme. The Olympians folded after the 1953 season.

O'Brien's daughter, Kyle, was an All-State basketball player at North Central High and, along with her father, is a member of the Indiana Basketball Hall of Fame. Kyle was a member of North Central's two-time state champion golf team and was medalist in 1975. She went on to become national Collegiate Player of the Year at Southern Methodist University (SMU) and was the Ladies Professional Golf Association Rookie of the Year in 1981. She later was golf coach at SMU.

68 | IU BACKS OUT OF HOOSIER CLASSIC

IT WASN'T A TOURNAMENT, IT was a classic.

They called it the Hoosier Classic, and in the late '40s and '50s, it was a popular holiday event featuring basketball teams from Butler, Indiana, Purdue, and Notre Dame. The fans loved it, but Indiana coach McCracken didn't.

McCracken didn't like the fact that the two-night classic was held every year on Butler's home court, never mind that IU enjoyed the biggest proportion of the crowd. He noted that Hurryin' Hoosiers fans always expected an Indiana victory. Indiana had extremely strong teams during that era, winning the NCAA title in 1953 and posting a 20–4 record in 1954. In fact, Indiana won four Big Ten championships in six years. But after the Bulldogs beat the Hoosiers in both the 1957 and '58 classics and lost to IU by only 6 points in December 1959, McCracken pulled his team out of the event.

The other schools tried to keep the event alive by bringing in Illinois to replace IU in 1960—Butler won that year by beating both Purdue and Illinois by 2 points—but the substitution was not enough to save the event and it was discontinued.

Because Big Ten members IU and Purdue already played each other in the regular season, they could not meet in the Hoosier

Classic. Each team played Butler and Notre Dame annually, and a champion was declared only if the same team won both games.

The Bulldogs won the first four Hoosier Classics, beating both Purdue and IU in the 1947–48 and 1948–49 seasons. In 1949 and '50 they beat Purdue but lost to IU. After the 1951–52 classic, it was abandoned until being reinstated in December 1957.

Because the Hoosier Classic involved little travel, it was profitable for all four teams. Some of the top players of that era participated, including Terry Dischinger, Walt Bellamy, Archie Dees, Buckshot O'Brien, Bobby Plump, Don Schlundt, Bob Leonard, Bill Garrett, and Tom Hawkins.

A similar tournament featuring Butler, Indiana, Purdue, and Notre Dame was launched in December 2012 as the Crossroads Classic. Unlike the Hoosier Classic, these games were played on a neutral court at Bankers Life Fieldhouse in Indianapolis.

69 | TONY AT PURDUE?

PURDUE COACH TONY HINKLE.

Or, Indiana coach Tony Hinkle.

Neither has a proper ring to it—at least not to Butler fans, for whom the thought of their beloved former coach on the campus of another in-state rival is repulsive.

Nonetheless, Butler's Hall of Fame mentor, who died in 1992, had offers to coach the Boilermakers and the Hoosiers and turned them both down. He said Purdue approached him two or three times, but Tony's heart always bled Butler blue. As driven as he was to be a successful basketball coach, he didn't want to find that success somewhere else.

Today, successful coaches at smaller colleges usually receive offers they can't refuse. If a basketball power wants a coach badly enough, no offer is too large. "Everyone has his price" is the saying, but Hinkle didn't.

Shortly before retiring as the Bulldogs coach in 1970, Hinkle told the *Indianapolis Star* that both Purdue and IU had talked to him about moving. So had Butler's Big Ten rivals Minnesota and Michigan.

"But there was no reason to leave Butler," Hinkle said.[1] "Back in those days we had as fine a facilities as anyone in the United States. We were a pioneer in building a fieldhouse. Nobody had anything like it. We were getting good crowds going on trips, doing everything in a big fashion.

"Our ambitions were such that we tried the Missouri Valley Conference, then we tried the Mid-America Conference." The Bulldogs had joined the MVC in 1932 but left two years later. They were members of the MAC from 1946 to 1949.

Instead of taking more glamorous jobs elsewhere, Hinkle simply took on many jobs at Butler. He started as baseball coach in 1921, became basketball coach in 1926, became athletic director in 1931, and was named football coach in 1935.

Tony had an unpleasant experience when he first arrived at Butler in 1921. Harlan "Pat" Page, his basketball coach at the University of Chicago, had asked him to come assist him and coach the freshmen at Butler.

Hinkle asked for the blessing of Chicago legend Amos Alonzo Stagg but never heard back from him, so he took the new job. Later, Stagg, who died in 1965 at age 102, was highly critical of Hinkle for taking the job, which paid very little. "We were scared of [Stagg]. When we saw him coming down the sidewalk, we would cross the street so we wouldn't have to speak," Hinkle told the *Star*.

There was a time when Hinkle's stature at Butler wasn't so high. As head coach of the football team in 1926, his team went 3–6. The administration replaced him with George "Potsy" Clark, a well-known player at Illinois alongside future NFL star Harold "Red" Grange. Tony was demoted to assistant coach.

As Hinkle told the *Star*, "I didn't have the name they wanted to open the new stadium. They wanted a big name." At the time, Butler was envisioning a big-time athletic program. There was talk of building more than thirty thousand seats in Butler Bowl and the fifteen-thousand-seat fieldhouse was under construction, set to open in 1928. Jordan Hall also was opened in 1928.

70 | HINKLE AND THE ORANGE BASKETBALL

HINKLE WILL NEVER BE REMEMBERED for fashion. He was known for wearing white socks with his coat and tie. Like O. J. Simpson, he would never have been caught dead wearing those "ugly ass" Bruno Magli shoes[1]—that is, if he'd ever heard of them. Tony's clothing was as dated as the underhand free throw, yet he was responsible for modernizing the basketball.

Basketballs originally came in various shades of brown, which Hinkle thought made them hard for large crowds to see well. According to Howard Caldwell, author of Hinkle's biography, *Tony Hinkle: Coach for All Seasons*, Tony suggested basketballs be colored orange, and the Spalding sporting goods company designed balls of that color.[2] They were tested during practices at a Final Four in Louisville in the late 1950s, and the NCAA was sufficiently impressed to adopt the new ball design the following year.

71 | NORM ELLENBERGER'S VARIED CAREER

NORM ELLENBERGER WAS A LEGEND in New Mexico years after he was a three-sport star at Butler.[1] In a way, he was a man who led three lives: a basketball, football, and baseball standout with the Bulldogs; a coach whose sideline demeanor earned him the nickname "Stormin' Norman"; and a veteran coach who enjoyed coaching girls' basketball as much as he did national contenders.

His first and third lives were set apart from any controversy. The middle one saw him linked to a cheating scandal at the University of New Mexico that smeared his name.

Ellenberger's days at Butler were special. He was captain and All-Conference honoree in football and starred as a halfback on one of Butler's better teams. He pitched a no-hitter in baseball and played briefly in the Pittsburgh Pirates organization. He taught seven years at New Haven High, his alma mater. He was coach at Monmouth College for three seasons, leaving in 1967 to become assistant basketball coach at New Mexico. In 1972 Ellenberger was appointed the head coach there.

Under his direction, the Lobos won the Western Athletic Conference title in 1974 and 1978, and his teams compiled a record of 134–62. Ellenberger, wearing mod clothing and sporting bushy hair, became a celebrity in Albuquerque and was lovingly known as Stormin' Norman. His world changed in 1979 when the school was cited with changing academic records and other misdeeds for which he was fired.

Despite the scandal, Ellenberger remained popular with Lobo fans, even to the point where some wanted him rehired. His image was also helped when he was later hired as an assistant by UTEP coach Don Haskins and Indiana's Bob Knight.

Ellenberger left Indiana in 2000 and joined the staff of the Chicago Bulls. During that period he fell in love with Michigan's Upper Peninsula and moved to that area, where he became coach of a girls' high school team. He enjoyed outstanding success there, being named Coach of the Year in three different districts.

He was mourned over the entire area when he died in November 2015 at age 83, two years after being inducted into Butler's Hall of Fame. The induction was delayed because some felt his New Mexico situation should have prevented it. The support of his high school players helped seal the deal, however.

72 | A RUGGED FIRST ROUND: BUTLER HOSTS FORMIDABLE SECTIONAL

FOR THE BASKETBALL JUNKIE, BUTLER Fieldhouse was the site of the best four days of competition the sport could offer. It traditionally began the last week of February and was called the Indianapolis Sectional. Things changed in 1974 when Indiana went to class basketball. Going forward, Indianapolis schools were sent to different sites depending on their school size and location.

At its height, the famous Indiana high school championship consisted of four weeks of play that pared more than seven hundred teams down to a single champion. The first week of games was distributed to sixty-four different sites around the state. Most of the sites averaged eight to twelve teams, and the sixty-four sectional winners advanced to four-team regionals the following Saturday. The sixteen regional winners went on to four-team semistate rounds, which determined the four teams in the state finals.

Butler Fieldhouse hosted games all four weeks, but it was the sectional at Butler that made it extraordinary for fans, not to mention unfair to the teams assigned to play there. "Ten of the largest schools in Indiana were all in one sectional," said Cox, a star at Broad Ripple. "Tech was the largest school in the state,

Manual was big, Broad Ripple had 1,750 students. Shortridge was big. Washington was big. Warren Central and Lawrence Central were in there. We cut each other's throats."

The Indianapolis Sectional started with three games on Wednesday night and three more on Thursday night. Games were played all day Friday to set up Saturday's semifinal games in the afternoon and the championship game at night.

Several Indianapolis teams might be rated each year, but only one had a chance of winning the state. No school from Indianapolis did so until Crispus Attucks in 1955. Tech made the championship game in 1929, 1934, and 1952. Attucks broke through with titles in '55, '56, and '59; Washington won in 1965 and '69; and Broad Ripple won the state in 1980.

"I played on a couple of pretty decent teams at Broad Ripple. We got to the third round once out of my three years," Cox recalled. "The other times we got beat in the first or second rounds."

Cox said he kidded his Butler teammate Plump about the alleged "easy" road Plump's Milan Indians had to their state championship. "I told Plump, 'If you guys had played in the Indianapolis Sectional, you probably wouldn't even gotten out of the sectional.' And he said, 'Bullshit, we were good.' And I said, 'You were good, but you got to the semistate before you had to play anybody.'"

* * *

A sidelight to the Milan story involves a Milan player named Kenny Delap. Delap was among the twelve players on the Milan roster all season, but when tournament play started, a team was limited to ten players in uniform. Most of the ten players who dressed are household words in many basketball circles.

"Kenny Delap was a junior on that team, and he couldn't get to the tournament, so he never gets recognized," said Cox. "My son married his daughter."

73 | WAS DAMPIER DRIVEN AWAY?

LOUIE DAMPIER WAS A PROTOTYPICAL Butler-style guard, small in stature with the soft touch of a mother's hands. He could shoot a basketball with anyone in the nation, and, as a high school star at Southport, he was experiencing the college recruiting process in 1963.

Normally, a player of Dampier's talent would have IU scouts clamoring outside his door. But the Hurryin' Hoosiers expressed only a passive interest in the six-foot Southport star. Purdue showed even less interest, but Butler's Hinkle wanted "Little Louie" after first seeing him play as a junior. He fit the mold of many previous Bulldogs.

Then, a Butler fan got involved in recruiting Dampier, and he was driven away not only from Butler but from all the other Indiana schools. Instead, Dampier enrolled at Kentucky and became an All-American guard on the No. 1 team in the nation.

Former Southport coach Carl "Blackie" Braden once told *Indianapolis News* sportswriter Corky Lamm that both IU and Purdue saw Dampier play only once.[1] So did Kentucky. Coach Adolph Rupp, apparently having made up his mind, left at halftime after seeing Louie make something like 9 of 10 shots.

According to Braden, Louie probably would have chosen Butler, but one of its "recruiters" was on him so much about the Bulldogs that Dampier got sick and tired of it. Thus, when Kentucky came calling, Louie visited the Lexington school, liked it, and enrolled.

In 1966 Rupp's Wildcats were unbeaten until the last game of the regular season when they were upset by Tennessee. With a starting lineup known as Rupp's Runts, they lost the national title in a classic game against Texas Western. Kentucky's lineup of Dampier, Pat Riley, Tommy Kron, Larry Conley, and Thad Jaracz earned their nickname because none of them stood taller than six feet five.

Now a Basketball Hall of Fame member, Dampier went on to play nine seasons for the Kentucky Colonels of the ABA, scoring 13,726 points. When the ABA merged into the NBA, he played three years with the San Antonio Spurs.

74 | ASSISTANT GETS THE JOB DONE: "WHAT'S SO TOUGH ABOUT NOTRE DAME?"

BOB DIETZ WAS AN ALL-AMERICAN basketball player at Butler in 1940 and later served as an assistant coach under Hinkle for twenty years. Plump tells a story about how Dietz became acting head coach when Hinkle had an operation and was laid up in the hospital for a time.

"We played Notre Dame, and we hadn't defeated Notre Dame at Notre Dame since the '30s. We beat them and [Ted] Guzek scored 38 and I had 32 because we could change off and they didn't play a zone," Plump said. "When Mr. Hinkle came back, we were all at center court, and Bob Dietz looked at him and said, 'So, what's so tough about Notre Dame, Hink?'"

75 | CHAD TUCKER IS STILL BUTLER'S TOP SCORER

CHAD TUCKER'S CAREER AT BUTLER spanned five years through 1988. His life spanned an all-too-short thirty-one years.

Tucker, the all-time scoring leader for the Bulldogs, overcame virtually every challenge he faced on the basketball court. It was the game of life that overcame him.

Tucker's 2,321 points remains the school record, and his 468 free throws trails only Matt Howard and Bobby Plump. His free-throw percentage was .827, among the top 10 in school history. The six-foot-eight forward from Cloverdale averaged 19.8 points a game for his career, second only to Billy Shepherd's 24.1.

Chad played for his father, Al Tucker, at Cloverdale and became addicted to basketball at a young age. Whatever disappointments he might have been experiencing in life always evaporated when he was near a basketball goal. He was a typical Hoosier kid, one who shot baskets morning, afternoon, and night.

Tucker made the Indiana All-Star team but wasn't heavily recruited. Butler and Murray State, coached by Terre Haute native Ron Greene, were the only schools to actively recruit him. When Chad became a Bulldog, he started as a freshman and made 62 percent of his shots. As a sophomore, he averaged almost 20 points a game and led Butler to an eight-game winning streak at the end of the season.

Tucker played only four games as a senior before separating his shoulder, but the NCAA granted him another season of eligibility during which he averaged 24 points a game.

Chad committed suicide in May 1996 after playing seven seasons professionally in Europe. He left a note that read, "What I have accomplished is nice. I'm proud, but what I've become I hate and can't accept."

Tucker was posthumously inducted into the Butler Athletic Hall of Fame in 2007 and the Indiana Basketball Hall of Fame in 2013.

76 | OSCAR WAS *THE* GUY

TO THE GENERATION THAT SAW him play at Crispus Attucks High, Robertson must have come from another planet. Raised in a part of town not far from Butler, he could have been the best Bulldog of all time. That's because he might be the best player of all time.

Crispus Attucks, an African American school adjacent to downtown Indianapolis, won the state championship in 1955 and '56, losing but once over both seasons. Oscar, with his reputation hardly needing a last name, wound up at the University of Cincinnati and the Basketball Hall of Fame. En route, he left his mark on Hinkle Fieldhouse.

Many of Attucks's games were played at Butler Fieldhouse, and its path to the state championships saw every tournament game played there. When he was a sophomore, Oscar faced off against Plump and the Milan Indians.

Plump, two years older, outscored Robertson 28–22 as Milan beat Attucks 65–52 and advanced to the state finals. Milan, featuring five-foot-eleven center Gene White, ran what North Carolina later claimed to have invented, the four-corner offense.

"We had heard of Oscar, obviously," Plump said years later. "Within two or three minutes into the game, you knew who *the* player was. I mean, he was so much better than anybody on the floor. The only reason he had only 22 was we kept the ball away from him so much. Oscar, even as a sophomore, saw the whole game, and when you were playing against him, you knew he was *the* guy. There was no question."

Plump said Robertson is one of the players who would have transcended into the modern generation.

Milan and Attucks nearly crossed paths in 1953, but Attucks, led then by Oscar's older brother, Bailey, and Hallie Bryant, was upset by Shelbyville in the afternoon round of the Indianapolis Semistate. Milan beat Shelbyville at night to advance to the state finals, where it lost to South Bend Central in the afternoon.

Muncie Central, featuring the same starting five that lost to Milan in the 1954 championship game, lost a close battle to Attucks the following year. Oscar's interception of a long pass preserved the Tigers' lead in the waning seconds.

77 | REMEMBERING ANDREW SMITH, JOEL CORNETTE, AND EMERSON KAMPEN IV

TWO THOUSAND SIXTEEN WAS A painful year for the Butler family, which lost three of its own within an eight-month period.

Butler folks stick together, whether on the court, in the stands, or in life. Andrew Smith's lengthy fight against cancer triggered supporters' deepest emotions for many months preceding his death at age 25 on January 12, 2016.

Smith faced a two-year battle with cancer after playing four seasons at Butler, where his team reached the national championship games in 2010 and 2011. His battle was well documented on the website "Kicking Cancer with the Smiths," written affectionally by his wife, Sam.

The passing of 35-year-old Joel Cornette from coronary artery disease on August 16, 2016, was more sudden but no less horribly felt by those who watched him, as they did with Smith, battle for the Bulldogs in Hinkle Fieldhouse. Cornette was a member of Butler's 2003 Sweet Sixteen team and made a last-second dunk to beat Indiana. The Bulldogs won 100 of 130 games during his four years.

Sandwiched between these two blows was another tragedy. Emerson Kampen IV, the eight-month-old son of Emerson and Kylie Kampen, died of Leigh's Disease, a genetic disease that claimed his life on February 1, 2016, about three months after he was diagnosed. He was known to the Bulldogs as "Little Em." His father, a former Butler center (2008–13), is now an assistant coach for LaVall Jordan.

78 | STEVEN'S DISCIPLE NORED SHOWS CHARACTER AND PROMISE

STEVENS BECAME THE BASKETBALL WORLD'S poster boy in 2010 when he coached Butler to the national championship game as a 33-year-old. If some college is thinking about hiring another young coach with great potential, it might want to look at Ronald Nored.

Nored is a disciple of Stevens. He was a starter on the Bulldogs' first Final Four team and a coach as soon as he graduated from college. As a point guard, he had already been a coach on the floor, a player who put great emphasis on defense and a clutch performer of the first order.

Purdue coach Matt Painter expressed his admiration for Nored after Ronald was asked to come off the bench during Butler's second trip to the Final Four in 2011. A reporter asked Nored if he was disappointed at his reserve role after having been a starter.

Nored's response, as Painter recalled, was, "I didn't come to Butler to start, I came to Butler to win."

Nored almost didn't come to Butler at all. He had committed to play at Western Kentucky, but a coaching change there led him to reconsider.[1] A native of Homewood, Alabama, Nored turned down an academic scholarship to Harvard and on arriving at

Butler was voted class president. His leadership qualities were evident when he started every game as a freshman.

Immediately after graduation he was hired as basketball coach at Brownsburg High near Indianapolis. He had a brief stint under former Butler assistant Matt Graves at South Alabama, and then Stevens offered him a coaching position with the Boston Celtics organization. Nored split his time as an assistant coach with the Maine Red Claws of the NBA Development League and as player development coach of the Celtics.

In 2014 he was named Player Development Director for Boston in charge of off-the-court development. He spent the 2015–16 season as an assistant coach at Northern Kentucky University. In 2017 he coached the Brooklyn Nets' G League development league team.

79 | BUTLER'S NATIONAL CHAMPIONSHIPS

DID YOU KNOW THAT BUTLER University has a national championship to its credit? Actually, it has two of them.

Well, sort of.

The first NCAA Tournament wasn't held until 1939, when Oregon defeated Ohio State for the title. How did they determine the national champion before that? Not very efficiently, it would appear.

In 1924 Butler went to the AAU National Tournament in Kansas City, Missouri, and after winning four games there against suspect competition, the Bulldogs were declared national champions.

Butler defeated Schooley-Woodstock 34–29 in its opening game, then beat the Hillyards by the almost identical score of 35–29. That pitted the Bulldogs against Kansas State Teachers, and they rolled to an easy 40–21 victory, earning a berth in the championship game. Butler won that game over the Kansas City Athletic Club, 30–26. The Bulldogs, coached by Harlan Page, had only a 7–7 record entering the tournament, losing four of their first five games. They closed the regular season with five wins in their last six games.

The season included victories over Chicago, Marquette, Hanover, and Franklin and losses to Iowa and Wisconsin.

Three years later Hinkle took over as coach, and his first team went 17–4 with two wins over Michigan State, DePaul, and Marquette. Hinkle's 1929 team was even better with a 17–2 record that featured victories over Purdue, North Carolina, Illinois, and Notre Dame. At the end of that season, Butler was awarded the John J. McDevitt Trophy, symbolic of another national championship, by the Veteran Athletes of Philadelphia.

80 | BACK IN THE OLD DAYS

BUTLER HAS PLAYED APPROXIMATELY 270 different opponents since it began basketball competition in 1892. No results are available for the first three seasons, although the names of the early Bulldogs are on file. According to the 2018 *Butler Media Guide*, the first Butler players were George Anderson, Charles Baker, Harry Griffith, Henry Griffith, Keith Hummell, John Kettenbach, John Lister, Harold Poer, David Smith, Luther Thompson, and Frank Williams.[1]

The first names of several other players remain unknown: Davidson, Hall, Hynes, Ormes, Robinson, Shakleton, Sommerville, and Wright.

The first Butler game on record was a 13–1 victory over the YMCA in 1896 or '97. The following season saw Butler go 2–3 while coached by James Zink. Butler lost to Indiana 22–6, beat Rose Polytechnic 18–0, lost to Miami of Ohio 6–0, shut out Earlham College 18–0, and lost to the Indianapolis Athletic Club 14–0.

The IU archives make no mention of the 1896 game against Butler. The Hoosiers record their first season as 1900–01 and list them losing the first two games in their history to Butler, 20–17 and 29–24. More than a century later, Butler lists its all-time record against IU as 70–57 in favor of the Hoosiers.

81 | BENEATH THE HOOSIER SKY

THE *BUTLER WAR SONG* WAS largely unknown nationwide until the Bulldogs reached the Final Four in 2010, but its recognition factor has increased as the team has played, and won, more intersectional games. The school fight song, written by John Heiney, Class of 1923, goes as follows:

We'll sing the Butler War Song,
We'll give a fighting cry;
We'll fight the Butler battle
. . . Bulldogs ever do or die.
And in the glow of the victory firelight,
History cannot deny
To add a page or two
For Butler's fighting crew
Beneath the Hoosier sky.

ENDNOTES

Preface and Acknowledgments

1. Barry Collier, Butler University Press Conference. Indianapolis, IN, November 2, 1993.
2. Unattributed newspaper clipping from Butler archives.

1. Hinkle Is Home Away from Home for IU Fans

1. Jim McGrath, interview by author, December 8, 2016. Unless otherwise noted, all quotes attributed to McGrath are from this interview.
2. David Benner, "Trice 'n Guice Put Indiana on Ice," *Indianapolis Star*, November 28, 1993.
3. Barry Collier, interview by author, January 4, 2017. Unless otherwise noted, all quotes attributed to Collier are from this interview.

3. Graves and Green: "Fire and Ice"

1. Brandon Crone, interview by author, January 3, 2017. Unless otherwise noted, all quotes attributed to Crone are from this interview.
2. Terry Johnson, interview by author, January 3, 2017. Unless otherwise noted, all quotes attributed to Johnson are from this interview.

4. It's a Dog's World at Butler

1. Michael Kaltenmark, interview by author, January 1, 2017. Unless otherwise noted, all quotes attributed to Kaltenmark are from this interview.

2. Brendan Prunty, "Final Four: Butler Mascot Blue II Has Become a Star in His Own Right," *Star-Ledger*, April 2, 2011, http://www.nj.com/college-basketball/index.ssf/2011/04/final_four_butler_mascot_blue_ii_has_become_a_star_in_his_own_right.html.

6. Bulldogs Pound Wake Early

1. Nick Gardner, interview by author, January 16, 2017. Unless otherwise noted, all quotes attributed to Gardner are from this interview.

9. Help Is on the Way

1. Pat Forde, "Hayward, Butler Hitting on All Cylinders," ESPN.com, February 20, 2010, http://www.espn.com/mens-college-basketball/columns/story?columnist=forde_pat&id=4930939.

11. Ronald Nored Sticks to Steph Curry

11. Pat Forde, "How Stephen Curry Went from Ignored College Recruit to Possible NBA MVP," Yahoo Sports, April 24, 2015, https://sports.yahoo.com/news/how-stephen-curry-went-from-ignored-college-recruit-to-possible-nba-mvp-011555328.html.

14. "Plump Doesn't Need a Stunt Double—Exactly"

1. Bobby Plump, interview by author, June 16, 2017. Unless otherwise noted, all quotes attributed to Plump are from this interview.

15. A David-and-Goliath Story

1. For a transcript, see "NCAA Men's Final Four," ASAP Sports, April 4, 2010, http://www.asapsports.com/show_interview.php?id=62636.

2. William C. Rhoden, "Once the Underdog, Duke Is Now the Villain: 'The Most Eagerly Anticipated Championship Game in Years,'" *New York Times*, April 4, 2010.

16. Coming Down Off the Mountain

1. Chris Holtmann, interview by author, April 12, 2017. Unless otherwise noted, all quotes attributed to Holtmann are from this interview.

20. All in the Family

1. The details of Vanzant's story are from Michael Marot, "Butler's Vanzant Keeps Final Four Trip in Family," *USAToday*, March 31, 2011.
2. Quoted in Marot, "Butler's Vanzant Keeps Final Four Trip in Family."

23. Jones Is One of a Kind

1. Matt Painter, Purdue University press conference (Indianapolis, December 19, 2016). Unless otherwise noted, all quotes attributed to Painter are from this press conference.

24. Clarke's Stay Is Brief, but Brilliant

1. Andy Katz, "Rotnei Clarke Saga Ends with Transfer," Andy Katz Blog, ESPN, June 21, 2011. http://www.espn.com/mens-college-basketball/blog/_/name/katz_andy%20/id/6689307/plenty-blame-rotnei-clarke-transfer-drama-college-basketball.
2. Kelli Anderson, "Butler's Rotnei Clarke Learns Valuable Lesson After Scary Injury," *Sports Illustrated*, January 25, 2013, https://www.si.com/college-basketball/2013/01/25/rotnei-clarke-butler.

27. Worse Than a Death in the Family

1. Billy Witz, "Butler's Coach: Competitiveness Wrapped in Calm," *New York Times*, March 28, 2010, http://www.nytimes.com/2010/03/29/sports/ncaabasketball/29butler.html?emc=eta1.

28. Barlow's Floater Dooms Hoosiers

1. Chase Howell, "Walk-On Part in a Thriller," *Cincinnati Enquirer*, December 19, 2012, C6.
2. Michael Pointer, "Butler's Barlow Keeps Proving Doubters Wrong," *Indianapolis Star*, January 24, 2015, https://www.indystar.com/story/sports/college/butler/2015/01/24/former-walk-on-more-than-holds-his-own-in-brutal-big-east/22273183/.

35. Dawgs Knock Off No. 1 Wildcats Three Times

1. Jay Wright, Villanova press conference (Indianapolis, IN, January 4, 2017).
2. Ryan Pedon, interview by author, April 17, 2017.

36. Has Butler's Rise Affected IU?

1. Bob Knight. *The Dan Patrick Show*, March 10, 2017.

39. Kelan Martin Strong in Any Role

1. Tom Crean, Indiana University press conference (Bloomington, IN, December 16, 2016).

43. Talent Is Everywhere, Just Find It

1. Ed Cooley, Providence College press conference (Indianapolis, IN, January 1, 2017).
2. Mike Schrage, interview by author, January 3, 2017.
3. Unattributed clipping from Butler archives.

44. Hinkle Fieldhouse: A Historic Site

1. Bob Cook, "'Hoosiers' Turns 25," Forbes.com, November 21, 2011, https://www.forbes.com/sites/bobcook/2011/11/21/hoosiers-turns-25/#223a7e1417df.

46. Stevens Leads by Example

1. Matt Norlander, "College Coaches to NBA: How They've Fared the Past 20 Years," CBSsports.com, July 3, 2013, https://www.cbssports.com/college-basketball/news/college-coaches-to-nba-how-theyve-fared-the-past-20-years/.
2. Ben Dowsett, "Brad Stevens: Elite Coach and Boston's Safest Asset," Basketball Insiders, February 25, 2016, http://www.basketballinsiders.com/brad-stevens-bostons-safest-asset/.
3. Quoted in Dowsett, "Brad Stevens."
4. Kevin Connors, postgame comments, ESPN2, May 21, 2017.

5. Avery Bradley, Boston Celtics postgame press conference (Cleveland, OH, May 21, 2017).
6. Marcus Smart, Boston Celtics postgame press conference (Cleveland, OH, May 21, 2017).

48. "On the Ground Floor of Integration"

1. Wally Cox, interview by author, January 30, 2017. Unless otherwise noted, all quotes attributed to Cox are from this interview.
2. Tom Graham and Rachel Graham Cody, *Getting Open: The Unknown Story of Bill Garrett and the Integration of College Basketball* (New York: Atria Books, 2006).

49. Archey's 85 Straight Free Throws

1. Some of the information in this chapter is from Butler University, *Butler Basketball Media Guide, 2016–2017* (Indianapolis: Butler University, 2016), p. 67.

54. The Bulldogs' First NIT Trip

1. Mr. Basketball is named every season to honor someone voted to be the state's best player. The award is common in most states.

55. Butler Wins a Pair in Its First NCAA Tournament

1. Unattributed newspaper clipping from Butler archives.
2. Ibid.

56. You Want to Come to Butler, Kid?

1. Original in Plump's possession.

58. Fun Days in the ICC

1. Former Indiana sports information director, the late Tom Miller, told this story.

64. Bevo Francis Played Here—Once

1. Daniel Slotnik, "Bevo Francis Dies at 82; Scored 116 and 113 Points in College Basketball Games," *New York Times*, June 4, 2015, https://www.nytimes.com/2015/06/05/sports/basketball/bevo-francis-dies-at-82-scored-113-points-in-college-basketball-game.html.

65. Tony's Last Game

1. Bob Collins, *Indianapolis Star*, February 24, 1970.

69. Tony at Purdue?

1. Hinkle quotes in this chapter are from unattributed newspaper clippings from Butler archives.

70. Hinkle and the Orange Basketball

1. Peg Tyre, "Thanks to O.J., Bruno Maglis Are Really Big Shoes," *CNN Interactive*, January 23, 1997, http://www.cnn.com/US/9701/23/shoe.sales/.

2. Howard Caldwell, *Tony Hinkle: Coach for All Seasons* (Indianapolis: Indiana University Press, 2010).

71. Norm Ellenberger's Varied Career

1. Mark Smith, "Lobos Went Stormin' with Norman," *Albuquerque Journal*, June 23, 2013, https://www.abqjournal.com/239865/lobos-went-stormin-with-norman.html.

73. Was Dampier Driven Away?

1. Undated newspaper clipping from Butler archives.

75. Chad Tucker Is Still Butler's Top Scorer

1. Michael Pointer, "Chad Tucker Is Gone, But He's Still No. 1 at Butler," *Indianapolis Star*, January 18, 2015, https://www.indystar.com/story/sports/college/butler/2015/01/17/schools-all-time-leading-scorer-took-his-own-life-but-his-family-uses-it-to-teach-others/21778093/.

78. Steven's Disciple Nored Shows Character and Promise

1. Cory Wright, "Nored to Lead LI Nets," *NBA G League*, July 13, 2016, http://longisland.gleague.nba.com/news/unique-nored-to-lead-li-nets/.

80. Back in the Old Days

1. Butler University, *Butler Basketball Media Guide, 2017–2018* (Indianapolis, IN: Butler University, 2017).

REFERENCES

Anderson, Kelli. "Butler's Rotnei Clarke Learns Valuable Lesson After Scary Injury." *Sports Illustrated*, January 25, 2013. https://www.si.com/college-basketball/2013/01/25/rotnei-clarke-butler.

Benner, David. "Trice 'n Guice Put Indiana on Ice." *Indianapolis Star*, November 28, 1993.

Bradley, Avery. Boston Celtics Postgame Press Conference. Cleveland, OH, May 21, 2017.

Branch, John. "It's the Bricks That Make Butler Basketball Special." *New York Times*, March 17, 2010, B-11.

Butler University. *Butler Basketball Media Guide, 2017–2018*. Indianapolis, IN: Butler University, 2017.

———. *Butler Basketball Media Guide, 2016–2017*. Indianapolis, IN: Butler University, 2016.

Caldwell, Howard. *Tony Hinkle: Coach for All Seasons*. Indianapolis: Indiana University Press, 2010.

Clarke, Liz. "Blue II Has Taken Houston by Storm." *Washington Post*, April 3, 2011. https://www.washingtonpost.com/sports/blue-ii-has-taken-houston-by-storm/2011/04/03/AFw3XwXC_story.html?utm_term=.4cd05a83c906.

Collier, Barry. Butler University Press Conference. Indianapolis, IN, November 2, 1993.

———. Interview by author, January 4, 2017.

Cook, Bob. "'Hoosiers' Turns 25." Forbes.com, November 21, 2011. https://www.forbes.com/sites/bobcook/2011/11/21/hoosiers-turns-25/#223a7e1417df.

Collins, Bob. *Indianapolis Star*, February 24, 1970.

Cooley, Ed. Providence College Press Conference. Indianapolis, IN, January 1, 2017.
Cox, Wally. Interview by author, January 30, 2017.
Crean, Tom. Indiana University Press Conference. Bloomington, IN, December 16, 2016.
Crone, Brandon. Interview by author, January 3, 2017.
Dowsett, Ben. "Brad Stevens: Elite Coach and Boston's Safest Asset." *Basketball Insiders*, February 25, 2016. http://www.basketballinsiders.com/brad-stevens-bostons-safest-asset/.
Forde, Pat. "Hayward, Butler Hitting on All Cylinders." ESPN.com, February 20, 2010. http://www.espn.com/mens-college-basketball/columns/story?columnist=forde_pat&id=4930939.
———. "How Stephen Curry Went from Ignored College Recruit to Possible NBA MVP." Yahoo Sports, April 24, 2015. https://sports.yahoo.com/news/how-stephen-curry-went-from-ignored-college-recruit-to-possible-nba-mvp-011555328.html.
Gardner, Nick. Interview by author, January 16, 2017.
Graham, Tom, and Rachel Graham Cody. *Getting Open: The Unknown Story of Bill Garrett and the Integration of College Basketball*. New York: Atria Books, 2006.
Holtmann, Chris. Interview by author, April 12, 2017.
Howell, Chase. "Walk-On Part in a Thriller." *Cincinnati Enquirer*, December 19, 2012, C6.
Johnson, Terry. Interview by author, January 3, 2017.
Kaltenmark, Michael. Interview by author, January 1, 2017.
Katz, Andy. "Rotnei Clarke Saga Ends with Transfer." Andy Katz Blog, ESPN, June 21, 2011. http://www.espn.com/mens-college-basketball/blog/_/name/katz_andy%20/id/6689307/plenty-blame-rotnei-clarke-transfer-drama-college-basketball.
Knight, Bob. *The Dan Patrick Show*, March 10, 2017.
Marot, Michael. "Butler's Vanzant Keeps Final Four Trip in Family." *USAToday*, March 31, 2011.
McGrath, Jim. Interview by author, December 8, 2016.
"NCAA Men's Final Four." ASAP Sports, April 4, 2010. http://www.asapsports.com/show_interview.php?id=62636.
Norlander, Matt. "College Coaches to NBA: How They've Fared the Past 20 Years." CBSsports.com, July 3, 2013. https://www.cbssports.com/college-basketball/news/college-coaches-to-nba-how-theyve-fared-the-past-20-years/.

Painter, Matt. Purdue University Press Conference. Indianapolis, December 19, 2016.
Pedon, Ryan. Interview by author, April 17, 2017.
Plump, Bobby. Interview by author, June 16, 2017.
Pointer, Michael. "Butler's Barlow Keeps Proving Doubters Wrong." *Indianapolis Star*, January 24, 2015. https://www.indystar.com/story/sports/college/butler/2015/01/24/former-walk-on-more-than-holds-his-own-in-brutal-big-east/22273183/.
———. "Chad Tucker Is Gone, But He's Still No. 1 at Butler." *Indianapolis Star*, January 18, 2015. https://www.indystar.com/story/sports/college/butler/2015/01/17/schools-all-time-leading-scorer-took-his-own-life-but-his-family-uses-it-to-teach-others/21778093/.
Prunty, Brendan. "Final Four: Butler Mascot Blue II Has Become a Star in His Own Right." *Star-Ledger*, April 2, 2011. http://www.nj.com/college-basketball/index.ssf/2011/04/final_four_butler_mascot_blue_ii_has_become_a_star_in_his_own_right.html.
Rhoden, William C. "Once the Underdog, Duke Is Now the Villain: 'The Most Eagerly Anticipated Championship Game in Years.'" *New York Times*, April 4, 2010.
Schrage, Mike. Interview by author, January 3, 2017.
Slotnik, Daniel. "Bevo Francis Dies at 82; Scored 116 and 113 Points in College Basketball Games." *New York Times*, June 4, 2015. https://www.nytimes.com/2015/06/05/sports/basketball/bevo-francis-dies-at-82-scored-113-points-in-college-basketball-game.html.
Smart, Marcus. Boston Celtics Postgame Press Conference. Cleveland, OH, May 21, 2017.
Smith, Mark. "Lobos Went Stormin' with Norman." *Albuquerque Journal*, June 23, 2013. https://www.abqjournal.com/239865/lobos-went-stormin-with-norman.html.
Tyre, Peg. "Thanks to O.J., Bruno Maglis Are Really Big Shoes." *CNN Interactive*, January 23, 1997. http://www.cnn.com/US/9701/23/shoe.sales/.
Witz, Billy. "Butler's Coach: Competitiveness Wrapped in Calm." *New York Times*, March 28, 2010. http://www.nytimes.com/2010/03/29/sports/ncaabasketball/29butler.html?emc=eta1.
Woods, David. *The Butler Way: The Best of Butler Basketball*. Indianapolis, IN: Blue River, 2009.
———. *Underdawgs: How Brad Stevens and Butler University Built the Bulldogs for March Madness*. New York: Scribner, 2010.

ght, Cory. "Nored to Lead LI Nets." *NBA G League*, July 13, 2016. http://longisland.gleague.nba.com/news/unique-nored-to-lead-li-nets/.

Wright, Jay. Villanova Press Conference. Indianapolis, IN, January 4, 2017.

STAN SUTTON spent twenty-five years as a sportswriter at the *Courier-Journal* in Louisville, Kentucky, and is a member of the Indiana Sportswriters and Sportscasters Hall of Fame. This is his sixth book, all about sports. A native of Mays, Indiana, he spent his high school years in Shelbyville, Indiana. Sutton has worked for six daily newspapers in Indiana, Kentucky, and Ohio. He lives with his wife, Judy, in Bloomington, Indiana.

Printed and bound by CPI Group (UK) Ltd, Croydon, CR0 4YY

Printed and bound by CPI Group (UK) Ltd, Croydon, CR0 4YY

13/04/2025

14656542-0002